greatcasualfood

greatcasualfood

The Australian Women's **Weekly** cookbooks

contents

menu 1

Quick beetroot dip with sourdough

Red onion, cheese and vegetable frittata

Honey-vindaloo glazed chicken wings

Roast pumpkin, sesame and rocket salad

Summer berry and almond tart

Greek almond biscuits

casual food

When it comes to the modern approach to dining, formality has flown out the window. No-one has time to organise dinner parties anymore, and it's casual food that we serve to our friends nowadays. In the relaxed surroundings of informal gatherings, the pressure is off, as everyone pitches in to help the hosts prepare, serve and clear away the food. There are no longer any strict formulas as to the number of courses to serve when entertaining…
in fact, laying out platters and bowls of food in a casual help-yourself table arrangement is as widely practised as serving two or three delineated courses. One of the most popular – and casual – ways to entertain is to move the occasion outdoors. The surging popularity of barbecues and picnics is testament to that. Modern entertaining is, thankfully, a movable feast with no hard-and-fast rules. And what better place to move the feast than onto the picnic rug?

blanket food

Providing for a picnic can be as easy as going to your local delicatessen or supermarket. There, you'll be able to buy a host of marinated treats, such as olives, semi-dried tomatoes, roasted vegetables, artichoke hearts and fetta cheese, as well as a vast selection of fresh cheeses, cold meats (salami, prosciutto, shaved leg ham, etc), packaged dips like hummus, baba ghanoush, tzatsiki and taramasalata, as well as a variety of delicious breads.

If, however, you have the time to go to a little more trouble, consider using one of our three menu suggestions (opposite and below) – all of the recipes can be found within the pages of *Great Casual Food*.

menu 2

Baba ghanoush with turkish bread
Free-form spinach and ricotta pie
Teriyaki chicken wings
Spicy potato salad
Two-tomato salad
Fruit salad with honey yogurt
Little lime friands

menu 3

Ciabatta with olive and herb paste
Pumpkin, spinach and fetta frittata
Masala-crusted chicken wings
Baked ricotta with roasted capsicum salad
Portuguese custard tarts
Flourless chocolate hazelnut cake

picnic checklist

You'll never be caught short in the great outdoors if you use this picnic checklist.

- Esky and ice-bricks
- Tablecloth and napkins
- Picnic rug and/or weatherproof ground sheet
- Non-breakable plates, serving platters, cups and mugs
- Cutlery
- Corkscrew/bottle opener
- Salt shaker and pepper mill
- Sharp knives
- Chopping board
- Tongs
- Paper towels and plastic wrap
- Thermos of hot water
- Coffee, tea, milk and sugar
- Garbage bags
- Moist towelettes and tissues
- Leakproof containers for leftovers
- Insect repellent, sunscreen
- Small first-aid kit

breakfast & brunch

From Sunday morning scrambled eggs to delicious buckwheat pancakes with caramelised banana, the most important meal of the day is now one you'll really look forward to sharing with friends over a long, leisurely weekend morning.

buckwheat pancakes with caramelised banana

PREPARATION TIME **10 MINUTES (plus refrigeration time)**   COOKING TIME **20 MINUTES**

¼ cup (35g) self-raising flour
¼ cup (35g) buckwheat flour
1 tablespoon caster sugar
¼ teaspoon ground cinnamon
1 egg
¾ cup (180ml) skim milk
20g butter
¼ cup (50g) firmly packed brown sugar
4 medium bananas (800g),
  sliced thickly
2 tablespoons water

1 Combine flours, caster sugar and cinnamon in medium bowl; gradually whisk in combined egg and milk until smooth. Cover; refrigerate 30 minutes.

2 Meanwhile, melt butter in large frying pan. Add brown sugar; cook, stirring, until dissolved. Add banana and the water; cook, uncovered, stirring occasionally, about 2 minutes or until banana is caramelised.

3 Pour ¼ cup (60ml) of the batter into heated 20cm non-stick frying pan; cook pancake until browned both sides. Repeat with remaining batter to make four pancakes; cover to keep warm. Just before serving, halve each pancake; divide halves among serving plates. Spoon banana mixture onto each half; fold to enclose filling. Drizzle with remaining caramel sauce.

serves 4
per serving 6.1g fat; 1285kJ (307 cal)
tips Fresh strawberries may be used as a filling instead of caramelised bananas.
Dust pancakes with icing sugar mixture before serving.

toasted muesli

PREPARATION TIME **15 MINUTES**   COOKING TIME **45 MINUTES** (plus cooling time)

1 cup (90g) rolled oats
¼ cup (15g) unprocessed bran
¼ cup (35g) finely chopped dried apricots
¼ cup (20g) finely chopped dried apples
2 tablespoons sultanas
1 tablespoon honey
1 tablespoon water
1 cup (250ml) skim milk

1 Preheat oven to slow.
2 Combine oats, bran and fruit in medium bowl; stir in combined honey and water.
3 Spread mixture onto oven tray. Bake in slow oven about 45 minutes or until toasted, stirring occasionally; cool.
4 Serve muesli with milk, and fresh fruit, if desired.

serves 2
per serving 4.4g fat; 1433kJ (343 cal)
tip Muesli can be refrigerated in an airtight container for several weeks.

spanish tortilla

PREPARATION TIME **10 MINUTES**   COOKING TIME **15 MINUTES**

1 tablespoon olive oil
1 large brown onion (200g), sliced thinly
750g canned tiny new potatoes, drained, sliced thickly
6 eggs, beaten lightly
100g fetta cheese, chopped coarsely
⅓ cup (25g) finely grated parmesan cheese
⅓ cup (40g) coarsely grated cheddar cheese

1 Heat oil in medium frying pan; cook onion, stirring, until onion softens.
2 Combine onion, potato, egg and cheeses in large bowl.
3 Pour potato mixture into heated oiled medium non-stick frying pan.
   Cover; cook over low heat 10 minutes or until egg sets.
4 Carefully invert tortilla onto plate and slide back into frying pan.
   Cook further 5 minutes or until cooked through.
5 Remove from heat; allow to cool in pan. Serve with baby rocket,
   if desired.

serves 4
per serving 23.8g fat; 1560kJ (373 cal)
tip Tortilla can be eaten hot or cold and makes great picnic fare.

mini muffin dampers

PREPARATION TIME 10 MINUTES   COOKING TIME 25 MINUTES

3 cups (450g) self-raising flour
40g butter, chopped coarsely
1¾ cups (430ml) buttermilk
2 tablespoons basil pesto
¾ cup (90g) coarsely grated
**   cheddar cheese**
¼ teaspoon sweet paprika
1 tablespoon plain flour

1 Preheat oven to moderately hot. Grease 12-hole ⅓-cup (80ml) muffin pan.
2 Place self-raising flour in large bowl; rub in butter with fingertips. Using fork, stir in buttermilk to form a soft, sticky dough. Swirl pesto and cheese through; do not overmix.
3 Divide mixture among holes of prepared pan. Sprinkle with combined paprika and plain flour.
4 Bake in moderately hot oven 25 minutes.
5 Stand dampers in pan 5 minutes before turning out onto wire rack.

makes 12
per damper 7.8g fat; 929kJ (222 cal)
tip Use bottled pesto to save time. A sun-dried tomato pesto can also be used.

day-before muffins

PREPARATION TIME **15 MINUTES** (plus refrigeration time)   COOKING TIME **30 MINUTES**

⅔ cup (100g) coarsely chopped dried apricots
½ cup (95g) coarsely chopped dried figs
1⅓ cups (95g) All-Bran breakfast cereal
1½ cups (375ml) skim milk
1¼ cups (250g) firmly packed brown sugar
1½ tablespoons golden syrup
1¼ cups (185g) self-raising flour
½ cup (60g) pecans, chopped coarsely

1 Combine apricot, fig, cereal, milk, sugar and syrup in large bowl; mix well. Cover; refrigerate overnight.
2 Preheat oven to moderately hot. Lightly grease four holes only of a six-hole texas ¾-cup (180ml) muffin pan.
3 Stir flour and nuts into apricot mixture. Spoon mixture into prepared muffin pan; bake in moderately hot oven 30 minutes. Serve muffins hot or cold. Dust with sifted icing sugar and top with dried apricots, if desired.

serves 4
per serving 11.1g fat; 2941kJ (704 cal)
tip Muffins can be frozen for up to 2 months.

bircher muesli

PREPARATION TIME **15 MINUTES** (plus refrigeration time)

3 cups (270g) rolled oats
2 cups (500ml) fresh orange juice
400g yogurt
1 cup (160g) seeded dried dates, chopped coarsely
½ cup (85g) raisins
½ cup (150g) dried apricots, sliced thinly
⅓ cup (115g) honey
1 cup (250ml) milk
1 large apple (200g), peeled, grated coarsely
⅓ cup (45g) toasted slivered almonds

1   Combine oats, juice and yogurt in large bowl. Cover tightly; refrigerate overnight.
2   Stir dates, raisins, apricot, honey, milk and apple into oat mixture. Cover; refrigerate 30 minutes.
3   Serve muesli in individual serving bowls; top with almonds and fresh mixed berries, if desired.

serves 6
per serving 12.6g fat; 2000kJ (478 cal)
tips Try to find plain full-cream yogurt, sometimes called country-style or greek-style yogurt, for this recipe. Other types, especially the low-fat kind, are not suitable.
Additional milk can be added if muesli is too thick.
Use a tart, crisp green apple, such as a granny smith, for this recipe.

zucchini and mushroom omelette

PREPARATION TIME **10 MINUTES**   COOKING TIME **10 MINUTES**

10g butter
1 clove garlic, crushed
25g button mushrooms, sliced thinly
¼ cup (50g) coarsely grated zucchini
1 green onion, chopped finely
2 eggs
1 tablespoon water
¼ cup (30g) coarsely grated
**   cheddar cheese**

1 Heat half of the butter in small non-stick frying pan; cook garlic and mushroom, stirring, over medium heat about 2 minutes or until mushroom is lightly browned. Add zucchini and onion; cook, stirring, about 1 minute or until zucchini begins to soften. Remove vegetable mixture from pan; cover to keep warm.

2 Beat eggs and the water in small bowl. Add cheese; whisk until combined.

3 Heat remaining butter in same pan; swirl pan so butter covers base. Pour egg mixture into pan; cook, tilting pan, over medium heat until almost set.

4 Place vegetable mixture evenly over half of the omelette; using eggslice, flip other half over vegetable mixture. Using eggslice, slide omelette gently onto serving plate.

serves 1
per serving 29.2g fat; 1502kJ (359 cal)

banana bread

PREPARATION TIME **10 MINUTES**   COOKING TIME **30 MINUTES**

1¼ cups (185g) self-raising flour
1 teaspoon ground cinnamon
20g butter
½ cup (100g) firmly packed
**   brown sugar**
1 egg, beaten lightly
¼ cup (60ml) milk
½ cup mashed banana

1 Preheat oven to hot. Grease 14cm x 21cm loaf pan; line base with baking paper.

2 Sift flour and cinnamon into large bowl; rub in butter.

3 Stir in sugar, egg, milk and banana. Do not overmix, the batter should be lumpy. Spoon mixture into prepared pan. Bake in hot oven about 30 minutes or until cooked when tested; cool.

4 Cut bread into 12 slices; toast lightly. Spread each with a tablespoon of cream cheese and drizzle with a teaspoon of honey, if desired.

makes 12 slices
per slice 2.6g fat; 497kJ (119 cal)
tip Bread can be made a day ahead and is also suitable to freeze.

french toast

PREPARATION TIME **5 MINUTES**   COOKING TIME **10 MINUTES**

3 eggs, beaten lightly
$1/3$ cup (80ml) cream
$1/3$ cup (80ml) milk
¼ teaspoon ground cinnamon
1 tablespoon caster sugar
12 x 2cm slices french bread stick
50g butter

1 Combine egg, cream, milk, cinnamon and sugar in large bowl.
   Dip bread slices into egg mixture.
2 Melt half of the butter in large frying pan; cook half of the bread
   slices until browned both sides. Repeat with remaining butter
   and bread. Serve sprinkled with sifted icing sugar, if desired.

serves 4
per serving 25.1g fat; 1505kJ (359 cal)
tip This recipe is best made close to serving.

pumpkin, spinach and fetta frittata

PREPARATION TIME **10 MINUTES** COOKING TIME **35 MINUTES**

You will need a piece of pumpkin weighing approximately 800g for this recipe.

4 cups (640g) coarsely
  chopped pumpkin
1 large potato (300g), chopped coarsely
125g baby spinach leaves,
  chopped coarsely
200g fetta cheese, crumbled
¾ cup (90g) coarsely grated
  cheddar cheese
8 eggs, beaten lightly
1 small red onion (100g), sliced thinly

1 Preheat oven to very hot. Grease deep 23cm-square cake pan; line base and two opposite sides with baking paper.
2 Place pumpkin in large microwave-safe bowl. Cover; cook on HIGH (100%), stirring halfway through cooking time, about 5 minutes or until just tender. Place potato in small microwave-safe bowl. Cover; cook on HIGH (100%) 4 minutes or until just tender.
3 Combine pumpkin and potato in large bowl. Add spinach, cheeses and egg; stir to combine. Transfer egg mixture to prepared pan; top with onion.
4 Bake in very hot oven about 25 minutes or until firm. Stand 5 minutes before serving.

serves 4
per serving 30.6g fat; 2032kJ (486 cal)
tip If you don't have a microwave oven, boil or steam pumpkin and potato, separately, until just tender; drain.

scrambled eggs

PREPARATION TIME **3 MINUTES**   COOKING TIME **3 MINUTES**

4 eggs, beaten lightly
¹/₃ cup (80ml) milk
1 tablespoon finely chopped fresh chives
1 teaspoon butter

1 Place egg in small bowl with milk and chives; whisk to combine.
2 Melt butter in medium saucepan over low heat; add egg mixture. When egg mixture starts to "catch" on bottom of pan, stir continuously with wooden spoon. Cook only until egg is just firm. Serve with toasted brioche and smoked salmon, sprinkled with chopped fresh chives, if desired.

serves 2
per serving 15g fat; 837kJ (200 cal)
tips Whisk eggs just long enough to combine the yolks and whites; excessive beating will aerate the mixture too much.
Cook eggs just before serving.
Any chopped herb can be substituted for the chives.

buttermilk pancakes with ricotta cream

PREPARATION TIME **10 MINUTES** (plus standing time)
COOKING TIME **10 MINUTES**

1 cup (150g) self-raising flour
½ teaspoon ground cinnamon
1 tablespoon caster sugar
2 eggs, beaten lightly
1¼ cups (310ml) buttermilk
125g reduced-fat smooth ricotta cheese
½ cup (125ml) maple syrup
1 medium lemon (140g), cut into wedges

1 Sift flour, cinnamon and sugar into medium bowl. Whisk in combined egg and buttermilk, gradually, until smooth. Cover; stand 30 minutes.
2 Pour ¼ cup (60ml) of the batter into heated oiled non-stick frying pan; cook until bubbles start to appear. Turn pancake; cook until browned underneath. Remove pancake from pan; cover to keep warm. Repeat with remaining batter to make eight pancakes.
3 Combine ricotta with a tablespoon of the maple syrup in small bowl.
4 Serve pancakes with ricotta mixture, remaining maple syrup and lemon.

serves 4
per serving 7.6g fat; 1599kJ (382 cal)
tips This recipe is best made just before serving.
Pancakes are suitable to freeze.

porridge with apple compote

PREPARATION TIME **10 MINUTES**   COOKING TIME **15 MINUTES**

1 cup (90g) rolled oats
1 cup (250ml) skim milk
1½ cups (375ml) boiling water
2 tablespoons brown sugar

APPLE COMPOTE
2 medium apples (300g)
¼ cup (55g) caster sugar
¼ teaspoon ground cinnamon
¼ cup (60ml) water
8 dried apricots
1 tablespoon sultanas

1 Combine oats, milk and the water in medium saucepan; bring to a boil. Reduce heat; simmer, uncovered, about 5 minutes or until mixture thickens.
2 Serve porridge with apple compote, sprinkled with brown sugar.

apple compote Peel, core and slice apples thickly; combine apple with sugar, cinnamon and the water in medium saucepan. Cook, stirring, over low heat until sugar dissolves. Bring apple mixture to a boil. Reduce heat; simmer, uncovered 5 minutes. Add apricots and sultanas; simmer, uncovered, about 5 minutes or until apple is tender.

serves 4
per serving 2.1g fat; 1019kJ (244 cal)
tip Any other dried fruit, such as prunes, pears or peaches, may be used instead of the apricots.

fruit salad with honey yogurt

PREPARATION TIME **15 MINUTES**

¾ **cup (200g) low-fat yogurt**
2 tablespoons honey
200g peeled, coarsely
  chopped pineapple
200g seeded, peeled, coarsely
  chopped rockmelon
250g strawberries, halved
250g blueberries
1 large banana (230g), sliced thinly
2 tablespoons passionfruit pulp
2 teaspoons lime juice
12 fresh mint leaves

1 Combine yogurt and honey in small bowl.
2 Just before serving, combine remaining ingredients in large bowl;
   serve with honey yogurt.

serves 4
per serving 2g fat; 749kJ (179 cal)
tips Lime juice not only adds flavour to this recipe but also prevents
the banana from discolouring.
Honey yogurt can be made a day ahead and refrigerated, covered.

lime spritzer

PREPARATION TIME 10 MINUTES
COOKING TIME 5 MINUTES

½ cup (125ml) water
½ cup (110g) caster sugar
4 limes
1 tablespoon caster sugar, extra
ice cubes
1.25 litres (5 cups) soda water
2 sprigs fresh mint

1 Combine the water and sugar in small saucepan.
  Stir over heat, without boiling, until sugar dissolves;
  bring to a boil. Remove from heat; cool.
2 Cut each lime into eight wedges; place in large
  serving jug. Top with extra sugar.
3 Using the flat end of rolling pin, pound lime and
  sugar until well crushed. Add sugar syrup; stir well.
  Just before serving, add ice cubes, soda water and
  mint; stir gently.

  makes 1.75 litres (7 cups)
  per 250ml 0.06g fat; 315kJ (75 cal)
  tips Roll lime firmly on bench before pounding,
  to get maximum juice.
  Lime juice can be frozen.

spiced tea punch

PREPARATION TIME 20 MINUTES
COOKING TIME 10 MINUTES

1 litre (4 cups) water
4 tea bags
1 cinnamon stick
2 cardamom pods, bruised
4 whole cloves
1 cup (220g) caster sugar
1½ cups (375ml) cold water, extra
½ cup (125ml) fresh lemon juice
2 cups (500ml) fresh orange juice
1 medium lemon (140g), sliced thinly
¼ cup coarsely chopped fresh mint
1 litre (4 cups) mineral water
ice cubes

1 Bring the water to a boil in large saucepan; add tea bags,
  cinnamon, cardamom, cloves and sugar. Stir over low heat
  about 3 minutes or until sugar dissolves; discard tea bags.
  Refrigerate until cold.
2 Discard spices; stir in the extra water, juices, lemon and
  mint. Just before serving, add mineral water and ice cubes.

  makes 3 litres (12 cups)
  per 250ml 0.2g fat; 328kJ (91 cal)
  tips Tea mixture can be made a day ahead.

pineapple and mint frappé

PREPARATION TIME 20 MINUTES

1 large pineapple (2kg), peeled, chopped coarsely
40 ice cubes, crushed
1 tablespoon finely chopped fresh mint

1 Blend or process pineapple until smooth; transfer to large jug.
2 Stir in ice and mint; pour into serving glasses.

makes 1.5 litres (6 cups)
per 250ml 0.3g fat; 412kJ (99 cal)
tips Pineapple can be processed 3 hours ahead and refrigerated, covered, until ready to combine with ice and serve.
You can crush ice in a blender or food processor.

melon mania

PREPARATION TIME 10 MINUTES

You will need a piece of a small round watermelon weighing about 1.5kg and half of both a medium rockmelon and a honeydew melon for this recipe.

600g rockmelon, seeded, peeled, chopped coarsely
600g honeydew melon, seeded, peeled, chopped coarsely
1kg watermelon, seeded, peeled, chopped coarsely
250g strawberries, halved

1 Push fruit through juice extractor. Stir to combine.

makes 1 litre (4 cups)
per 250ml 1.1g fat; 603kJ (144 cal)
tip Refrigerate fruit before processing so the flavours are at their sharpest.

juices & frappés

finger food

These bite-size morsels are an ideal treat for any occasion.
Perfect to serve with drinks, or simply as an afternoon snack,
you'll find everything from skewered lemon prawns and
potato pizzettas to an assortment of tasty dips.

ciabatta with olive and herb paste

PREPARATION TIME **20 MINUTES**   COOKING TIME **10 MINUTES** (plus cooling time)

1 loaf ciabatta
2 tablespoons olive oil

OLIVE AND HERB PASTE
250g seeded green olives
$\frac{1}{2}$ small white onion (40g), chopped
freshly ground black pepper
1 clove garlic, crushed
$\frac{1}{4}$ cup (60ml) extra virgin olive oil
1 tablespoon coarsely chopped
**   fresh flat-leaf parsley**
1 teaspoon coarsely chopped
**   fresh oregano**
1 teaspoon lime juice

1   Preheat oven to moderately hot.
2   Cut bread into 1cm slices. Place bread in single layer on oven trays; brush with oil. Bake in moderately hot oven about 5 minutes on each side or until browned lightly and crisp; cool.
3   Serve ciabatta with olive and herb paste.

olive and herb paste   Process olives, onion, pepper and garlic into a coarse paste. Gradually add oil while motor is operating; stir in herbs and juice.

serves 6
per serving   19.4g fat; 1845kJ (441 cal)
tip   Recipe can be prepared a day ahead and refrigerated, covered separately.

potato pizzettas

PREPARATION TIME **15 MINUTES** (plus standing time)   COOKING TIME **30 MINUTES**

1.2kg old potatoes
80g butter, melted
¹⁄₃ cup (80g) bottled pesto
2 small cooked chicken breast fillets, sliced thinly
6 button mushrooms (60g), sliced thinly
1 cup (100g) grated mozzarella cheese
¹⁄₂ cup (40g) grated parmesan cheese
¹⁄₄ cup small fresh basil leaves

1 Preheat oven to hot. Peel potatoes; grate coarsely into medium bowl. Cover potato with cold water; stand 5 minutes. Drain potato well; squeeze to remove excess moisture. Place potato onto clean tea towel; pat dry.

2 Combine potato and butter in cleaned medium bowl; mix well.

3 Using 6.5cm round cutter as a guide, firmly press 1 level tablespoon of the potato mixture into cutter on baking paper covered oven tray. Repeat with remaining mixture, allowing about 2cm between discs.

4 Bake in hot oven 20 minutes. Turn; bake further 5 minutes or until discs are browned lightly.

5 Spread potato discs with pesto; top with chicken and mushroom. Sprinkle with combined cheeses; bake in hot oven about 5 minutes or until cheese melts.

6 Top with basil leaves to serve.

makes 24
per pizzetta 6.9g fat; 488kJ (116 cal)
tip Bases can be made 3 hours ahead. Topping is best added just before serving.

honey-vindaloo glazed chicken wings

PREPARATION TIME 15 MINUTES (plus marinating time)
COOKING TIME 40 MINUTES

24 chicken wings (approximately 2kg)
$^1/_3$ cup (115g) honey
2 tablespoons vindaloo curry paste
$^1/_3$ cup (80ml) soy sauce
2 tablespoons peanut oil

1 Cut chicken wings into three pieces at joints; reserve wing tips for another use.
2 Combine remaining ingredients in large bowl with chicken; toss to coat chicken in marinade. Cover; refrigerate 3 hours or overnight.
3 Preheat oven to hot. Place undrained chicken on oiled oven rack over baking dish; roast, uncovered, in hot oven about 40 minutes or until browned and cooked through, turning once during cooking.

makes 48
per piece 4.5g fat; 285kJ (68 cal)

masala-crusted chicken wings

PREPARATION TIME 15 MINUTES (plus marinating time)
COOKING TIME 45 MINUTES

1 tablespoon ground cumin
2 teaspoons ground coriander
1 teaspoon ground turmeric
$^1/_2$ teaspoon chilli powder
2 teaspoons garam masala
1 teaspoon finely grated lemon rind
2 tablespoons lemon juice
$^1/_4$ cup (60ml) peanut oil
24 chicken wings (approximately 2kg)

1 Heat medium dry frying pan; cook spices, stirring, over low heat until fragrant.
2 Combine spices in large bowl with rind, juice and oil.
3 Cut chicken wings into three pieces at joints; reserve wing tips for another use.
4 Add chicken to spice mixture; toss to coat chicken in marinade. Cover; refrigerate 3 hours or overnight.
5 Preheat oven to hot. Place undrained chicken on oiled oven rack over baking dish; roast, uncovered, in hot oven about 40 minutes or until browned and cooked through, turning once during cooking.

makes 48
per piece 4.8g fat; 273kJ (65 cal)

teriyaki chicken wings

PREPARATION TIME 20 MINUTES (plus marinating time)
COOKING TIME 40 MINUTES

24 chicken wings (approximately 2kg)
$^3/_4$ cup (180ml) teriyaki sauce
2 tablespoons peanut oil
2 teaspoons grated fresh ginger
2 cloves garlic, crushed
1 fresh red thai chilli, seeded, chopped finely
1 tablespoon brown sugar
1 teaspoon sesame oil
$^1/_2$ teaspoon five-spice powder
1 tablespoon sesame seeds, toasted

1 Cut chicken wings into three pieces at joints; reserve wing tips for another use.
2 Combine sauce, peanut oil, ginger, garlic, chilli, sugar, sesame oil and five-spice in large bowl with chicken; toss to coat chicken in marinade. Cover; refrigerate 3 hours or overnight.
3 Preheat oven to hot. Drain chicken; discard marinade. Place chicken on oiled oven rack over baking dish; roast, uncovered, in hot oven about 40 minutes or until browned and cooked through, turning once during cooking.
4 Serve chicken wings sprinkled with sesame seeds.

makes 48
per piece 4.6g fat; 268kJ (64 cal)
tips Reserved wing tips can be used to make stock. Marinated chicken can be prepared ahead and frozen in a sealed storage container or freezer bag for up to 6 months.

From left: masala-crusted chicken wings; teriyaki chicken wings; honey-vindaloo glazed chicken wings with garnish of rocket leaves

crystal prawns

PREPARATION TIME **15 MINUTES (plus standing time)** COOKING TIME **10 MINUTES**

1 medium carrot (120g)
1 trimmed stick celery (75g)
2 green onions
24 uncooked king prawns (1kg)
1 tablespoon dry sherry
1 tablespoon lemon juice
1 tablespoon peanut oil
$^{1}/_{4}$ cup (60ml) soy sauce

1 Cut carrot, celery and onions into long thin strips. Place vegetables in small bowl of iced water. Stand about 10 minutes or until they begin to curl; drain.

2 Shell prawns, leaving tails intact. To butterfly prawns, cut halfway through the back of each prawn. Remove vein; press flat.

3 Place prawns, sherry and juice in small bowl. Toss until combined; stand 10 minutes.

4 Heat oil in wok or large frying pan; cook prawns, in batches, until changed in colour. Serve prawns with vegetables and soy sauce.

serves 8
per serving 2.7g fat; 364kJ (87 cal)
tips Prawns can be butterflied 3 hours ahead. They are best when cooked just before serving.
Crystal prawns are so called because they look transparent if they are cooked properly.

prawn and crab wontons

PREPARATION TIME **1 HOUR**   COOKING TIME **30 MINUTES**

500g uncooked prawns
500g crab meat
1 teaspoon grated fresh ginger
1 clove garlic, crushed
4 green onions, chopped finely
1 tablespoon soy sauce
1 tablespoon sweet chilli sauce
80 wonton wrappers
1 tablespoon cornflour
1 tablespoon water
peanut oil, for deep-frying

DIPPING SAUCE
2 teaspoons soy sauce
2 tablespoons sweet chilli sauce
1 teaspoon dry sherry
1 green onion, chopped finely

1   Shell and devein prawns; chop prawn meat finely.
2   Combine prawn meat in medium bowl with crab, ginger, garlic, onion and sauces.
3   Place a heaped teaspoon of prawn mixture in centre of each wrapper. Brush edges with blended cornflour and water; pinch edges together to seal. Repeat with remaining wrappers, prawn mixture and cornflour paste.
4   Heat oil in large deep-frying pan; deep-fry wontons, in batches, until browned and cooked through. Drain on absorbent paper; serve with dipping sauce.

dipping sauce   Combine ingredients in small bowl.

makes 80
per wonton   0.9g fat; 348kJ (83 cal)
tip   Canned crabmeat can be used; drain well.
Frozen wontons can be deep-fried as is; freeze eight-wonton portions so you can take only as many as you need.

mini zucchini frittatas

PREPARATION TIME **20 MINUTES** COOKING TIME **15 MINUTES**

8 eggs
1 cup (240g) sour cream
$^1/_4$ cup finely chopped fresh chives
1 large yellow zucchini (150g), grated coarsely
1 large green zucchini (150g), grated coarsely
$^1/_3$ cup (25g) finely grated parmesan cheese
2 tablespoons coarsely chopped fresh chives, extra

1 Preheat oven to moderate. Lightly oil four 12-hole 1½-tablespoon (30ml) mini muffin pans.
2 Whisk eggs with two-thirds of the sour cream in large bowl until smooth; stir in chives, zucchini and cheese.
3 Divide mixture among holes of prepared pans. Bake, uncovered, in moderate oven 15 minutes; turn onto wire rack to cool. Top frittatas with remaining sour cream and extra chives.
4 Serve at room temperature.

makes 48
per frittata 3.1g fat; 142kJ (34 cal)
tips Frittata mixture can be prepared up to 2 hours ahead and baked just before serving. Cover; refrigerate until required.

deep-fried whitebait

PREPARATION TIME **10 MINUTES**   COOKING TIME **15 MINUTES**

1 cup (150g) plain flour
¹/₄ cup chopped fresh coriander
1 teaspoon garlic salt
500g whitebait
vegetable oil, for deep-frying

SPICED YOGURT DIP
10g butter
¹/₂ teaspoon ground cumin
¹/₂ teaspoon ground coriander
³/₄ cup (200g) yogurt
1 lebanese cucumber (130g), seeded,
   chopped finely
1 clove garlic, crushed
1 tablespoon lemon juice

1   Combine flour, coriander and garlic salt in large bowl. Add whitebait, in batches; toss until coated in mixture.
2   Heat oil in medium saucepan. Deep-fry whitebait, in batches, until browned and cooked through; drain on absorbent paper. Serve with spiced yogurt dip.

spiced yogurt dip   Heat butter in small saucepan. Cook cumin and coriander, stirring, until fragrant; cool. Combine yogurt, cucumber, garlic and juice in small bowl; stir in spice mixture.

serves 4
per serving   28.6g fat; 2083kJ (498 cal)

skewered lemon prawns

PREPARATION TIME 15 MINUTES (plus marinating time)   COOKING TIME 5 MINUTES

24 large uncooked king prawns (1.5kg)
¹/₃ cup (80ml) olive oil
1 tablespoon grated lemon rind
lemon wedges, to serve

1 Remove head and back vein from prawns. Remove legs, leaving shell intact. Cut along the underside length of prawn, without cutting all the way through. Thread prawns onto skewers.

2 Place prawns in large dish; pour over oil and lemon rind. Cover; marinate in refrigerator 3 hours.

3 Cook prawns on heated oiled grill plate (or grill or barbecue), flesh-side down, until browned lightly; turn. Cook until just cooked through; serve with lemon.

serves 8
per serving 9.7g fat; 686kJ (164 cal)
tips Recipe can be prepared 6 hours ahead.
You will need to soak 24 bamboo skewers in water for at least an hour before use, to prevent them from splintering and scorching.

spicy tomato salsa

PREPARATION TIME 10 MINUTES
COOKING TIME 15 MINUTES (plus cooling time)

4 medium tomatoes (760g), chopped finely
2 cloves garlic, crushed
1 small brown onion (80g), sliced thinly
1 teaspoon cajun seasoning
2 teaspoons no-added-salt tomato paste

1 Combine tomato with remaining ingredients in small saucepan.
2 Cook, stirring, about 15 minutes or until onion is soft and sauce has thickened; cool.

serves 4
per serving 0.4g fat; 153kJ (37 cal)
tip Salsa can be made 3 days ahead and refrigerated, covered.

quick beetroot dip

PREPARATION TIME 10 MINUTES

225g can sliced beetroot, drained well
¼ cup (70g) low-fat plain yogurt
1 teaspoon ground coriander
2 teaspoons ground cumin

1 Blend or process ingredients until well combined.

serves 4
per serving 0.6g fat; 137kJ (33 cal)
tip Dip can be made 3 days ahead and refrigerated, covered.

baba ghanoush

PREPARATION TIME 10 MINUTES (plus refrigeration time)
COOKING TIME 35 MINUTES (plus cooling time)

2 small eggplants (460g)
⅓ cup (95g) low-fat plain yogurt
1 tablespoon lemon juice
2 cloves garlic, crushed
1 teaspoon tahini
1 teaspoon ground cumin
½ teaspoon sesame oil
2 tablespoons chopped fresh coriander

1 Preheat oven to moderately hot.
2 Halve eggplants lengthways; place on oven tray. Bake in moderately hot oven about 35 minutes or until tender.
3 Cool; remove and discard skin. Blend or process eggplant with remaining ingredients until smooth. Cover; refrigerate 30 minutes.

serves 4
per serving 2.2g fat; 218kJ (52 cal)
tip Baba ghanoush can be made 3 days ahead and refrigerated, covered.

From front: quick beetroot dip; baba ghanoush; spicy tomato salsa

roast potatoes with aïoli

PREPARATION TIME **10 MINUTES**   COOKING TIME **40 MINUTES**

1kg tiny new potatoes, quartered
2 tablespoons olive oil
1 teaspoon sea salt
¹/₄ teaspoon hot paprika

AÏOLI
2 egg yolks
6 gloves garlic, peeled, quartered
1 teaspoon sea salt
³/₄ cup (180ml) olive oil

1 Preheat oven to very hot.
2 Combine potato, oil and salt in large baking dish. Roast, uncovered, in very hot oven about 40 minutes or until potato is browned and crisp. Sprinkle with paprika.
3 Serve potato with aïoli.

aïoli Blend or process egg yolks, garlic and salt until smooth. With the motor operating, gradually add oil; process until thick. A little lemon juice can be added to taste, if desired.

serves 10
per serving 21.3g fat; 1074kJ (256 cal)
tip The aïoli can be made a day ahead. The potatoes are best roasted just before serving.

grilled fetta

PREPARATION TIME **5 MINUTES**   COOKING TIME **5 MINUTES**

300g fetta cheese, halved
2 tablespoons olive oil
1 teaspoon chilli flakes
1 teaspoon dried oregano leaves

1 Place fetta on large sheet of foil; place on oven tray.
2 Combine oil, chilli and oregano in small bowl; drizzle over cheese. Grill about 5 minutes or until browned lightly. Stand 5 minutes; slice thickly.

serves 6
per serving 17.8g fat; 817kJ (195 cal)

gyoza with soy vinegar sauce

PREPARATION TIME **40 MINUTES (plus refrigeration time)**
COOKING TIME **15 MINUTES**

300g pork mince
2 tablespoons kecap manis
1 teaspoon sugar
1 tablespoon sake
1 egg, beaten lightly
2 teaspoons sesame oil
3 cups (240g) finely shredded chinese cabbage
4 green onions, sliced thinly
40 gyoza or gow gee wrappers
1 tablespoon vegetable oil

SOY VINEGAR SAUCE
$^1/_2$ cup (125ml) light soy sauce
$^1/_4$ cup (60ml) red vinegar
2 tablespoons white vinegar
2 tablespoons sweet chilli sauce

1 Combine pork, kecap manis, sugar, sake, egg, sesame oil, cabbage and onion in
    medium bowl; refrigerate 1 hour.
2 Place a heaped teaspoon of the pork mixture in centre of one wrapper; brush
    wrapper along one side of pork mixture with a little water. Pleat damp side of
    wrapper only; pinch both sides of wrapper together to seal. Repeat with
    remaining pork mixture and wrappers.
3 Cover base of large frying pan with water; bring to a boil. Add dumplings, in
    batches; reduce heat. Simmer, covered, 3 minutes; using slotted spoon, remove
    dumplings from pan. Drain and dry pan.
4 Heat vegetable oil in same pan; cook dumplings, in batches, unpleated side and
    base only, until golden brown.
5 Serve hot with soy vinegar sauce.

soy vinegar sauce Combine ingredients in small bowl.

makes 40
per gyoza 1.4g fat; 139kJ (31 cal)
per tablespoon sauce 0.1g fat; 35kJ (8 cal)
tip Gyoza filling can be prepared 4 hours ahead and refrigerated, covered.

empanadas

PREPARATION TIME **40 MINUTES**   COOKING TIME **45 MINUTES**

400g can tomatoes
1 tablespoon olive oil
1 medium brown onion (150g), chopped finely
1 clove garlic, crushed
1 teaspoon freshly ground black pepper
$^1\!/_2$ teaspoon ground cinnamon
$^1\!/_2$ teaspoon ground cloves
600g beef mince
$^1\!/_4$ cup (40g) raisins, chopped coarsely
1 tablespoon cider vinegar
$^1\!/_4$ cup (35g) toasted slivered almonds
2 x 800g packages ready-rolled quiche pastry
1 egg, beaten lightly
vegetable oil, for deep-frying

1 Blend or process undrained tomatoes until smooth; reserve.
2 Heat olive oil in large heavy-base saucepan; cook onion, garlic and spices, stirring, until onion is soft. Add beef; cook, stirring, until changed in colour. Drain away excess fat from pan. Stir in reserved tomato, raisins and vinegar; simmer, uncovered, about 20 minutes or until filling mixture thickens. Stir in nuts.
3 Cut 9cm rounds from each pastry sheet (you will get 32 rounds). Place a level tablespoon of the beef mixture in centre of each round; brush edge lightly with egg. Fold pastry over to enclose filling; press edges together to seal.
4 Heat vegetable oil in large deep-frying pan. Deep-fry empanadas until crisp and browned lightly; drain on absorbent paper. Serve immediately with a dollop of sour cream or bottled salsa, if desired.

serves 8
per serving 26g fat; 1664kJ (398 cal)
tip For a lower-fat version, empanadas can be baked, uncovered, in a preheated hot oven about 25 minutes or until browned.

cosmopolitan

PREPARATION TIME 5 MINUTES

10ml citron vodka
20ml vodka
30ml Cointreau
60ml cranberry juice
10ml fresh lime juice
1 cup ice cubes

1 Combine ingredients in a cocktail shaker. Shake
vigorously; strain into chilled glass.

glass 150ml cocktail
garnish a twist of lime rind

white russian

PREPARATION TIME 5 MINUTES

½ cup ice cubes
30ml vodka
30ml Kahlúa
30ml fresh cream

1 Place ice in glass; pour vodka then Kahlúa over ice.
Gently pour cream into glass over the back of a
tablespoon so cream floats; do not stir.

glass 180ml old-fashioned
garnish a straw

caipiroska

PREPARATION TIME 10 MINUTES

1 lime, cut into 8 wedges
1 tablespoon caster sugar
60ml vodka
½ cup ice cubes
½ cup crushed ice

1 Using a mortar and pestle, crush six lime wedges
   with sugar. Combine lime mixture in cocktail shaker
   with vodka and ice cubes; shake vigorously. Pour
   into glass with crushed ice; do not strain.

   glass 180ml old-fashioned
   garnish remaining lime wedges and two straws

passionfruit and pineapple daiquiri

PREPARATION TIME 5 MINUTES

45ml Bacardi
30ml passionfruit in syrup
30ml bottled pineapple juice
15ml Cointreau
15ml fresh lime juice
1 cup ice cubes

1 Combine ingredients in cocktail shaker; shake
   vigorously. Strain into chilled glass.

   glass 150ml cocktail
   garnish a piece of pineapple
   tip We used canned passionfruit in syrup, which
   is available from supermarkets.

starters

Every meal should begin with something delicious. Fresh rice paper rolls with prawns perhaps, or char-grilled polenta cakes? Whatever your preference, you'll find the perfect prelude to any main course here.

salt and pepper squid

PREPARATION TIME 15 MINUTES   COOKING TIME 5 MINUTES

500g squid hoods
³/₄ cup (110g) plain flour
1 tablespoon salt
1 tablespoon freshly ground
   black pepper
vegetable oil, for deep-frying
150g mesclun

CHILLI DRESSING
¹/₂ cup (125ml) sweet chilli sauce
1 teaspoon fish sauce
¹/₄ cup (60ml) lime juice
1 clove garlic, crushed

1   Cut squid in half lengthways; score inside surface of each piece. Cut into 2cm-wide strips.
2   Combine flour, salt and pepper in large bowl; add squid. Coat in flour mixture; shake off excess.
3   Heat oil in wok or large saucepan; deep-fry squid, in batches, until tender and browned all over. Drain on absorbent paper.
4   Serve squid on mesclun with chilli dressing. Serve with wedges of lime, if desired.

chilli dressing Combine ingredients in screw-top jar; shake well.

serves 4
per serving 12.2g fat; 1359kJ (325 cal)
tip Place flour, salt and pepper in a strong plastic bag with squid; grip the bag tightly closed, then gently shake to coat the squid in flour mixture. Remove squid from bag, shaking off any excess flour.

chilli scallops

PREPARATION TIME **15 MINUTES**   COOKING TIME **15 MINUTES**

1 tablespoon peanut oil
32 small scallops
4 cloves garlic, sliced thinly
50g fresh ginger, peeled, sliced thinly
2 fresh red thai chillies, seeded,
   chopped finely
3 green onions, sliced thinly
¹/₃ cup (80ml) sweet chilli sauce
1 teaspoon fish sauce
2 teaspoons brown sugar
¹/₂ cup (125ml) chicken stock
¹/₄ cup loosely packed, chopped
   fresh coriander

1   Heat half of the oil in wok or large frying pan; stir-fry scallops, in batches, until just changed in colour.

2   Heat remaining oil in wok; stir-fry garlic, ginger, chilli and onion until onion is soft.

3   Stir in combined sauces, sugar and stock; bring to a boil. Return scallops to wok; stir until heated through. Serve scallops sprinkled with coriander.

serves 4

per serving 6.1g fat; 585kJ (140 cal)

tips We used scallops with roe attached but the roe can be left out if you prefer. If you buy scallops in their shell, don't discard the shell, they are great (washed and dried) to use as serving "dishes".

You will need a piece of ginger about 5cm long for this recipe.

combination wonton soup

PREPARATION TIME **30 MINUTES**   COOKING TIME **10 MINUTES**

150g chicken mince
1 green onion, sliced thinly
2 tablespoons light soy sauce
16 wonton wrappers
24 medium uncooked prawns (600g)
1.5 litres (6 cups) chicken stock
100g chinese barbecued pork, sliced thinly
100g fresh shiitake mushrooms, sliced thinly
150g baby bok choy, chopped coarsely
4 green onions, sliced thinly, extra

1 Combine chicken, onion and half of the sauce in small bowl.
2 Place a heaped teaspoon of chicken mixture in centre of each wonton wrapper. Brush edges with a little water; pinch edges together to seal.
3 Shell and devein prawns, leaving tails intact.
4 Bring stock to a boil in large saucepan. Add wontons; cook, uncovered, about 3 minutes or until wontons are just cooked through.
5 Add prawns, remaining sauce, pork and mushroom; cook, uncovered, until prawns just change in colour. Add bok choy and extra onion; cook, uncovered, until bok choy just wilts.

serves 4
per serving 9.1g fat; 1155kJ (276 cal)
tip Uncooked wontons are suitable to freeze for up to 3 months. You don't have to defrost them; just remove from freezer and simmer in stock until cooked through.

baked ricotta with roasted capsicum salad

PREPARATION TIME **15 MINUTES**   COOKING TIME **30 MINUTES (plus standing time)**

200g low-fat ricotta cheese
2 tablespoons finely grated
   parmesan cheese
1 egg, beaten lightly
1 teaspoon coarsely chopped
   fresh sage
3 fresh bay leaves, chopped coarsely
2 medium red capsicums (400g)
2 medium yellow capsicums (400g)
250g mesclun
¼ cup (60ml) balsamic vinegar
1 tablespoon olive oil
1 tablespoon honey

1 Preheat oven to moderately slow.
2 Oil eight holes of a 12-hole ⅓-cup (80ml) non-stick muffin pan. Combine cheeses and egg in small bowl. Divide ricotta mixture among prepared holes; sprinkle with combined herbs.
3 Place muffin pan in large baking dish; add enough boiling water to come halfway up side of pan. Bake ricotta, uncovered, in moderately slow oven about 30 minutes or until set. Stand 10 minutes before turning ricotta out.
4 Meanwhile, quarter capsicums; remove and discard seeds and membranes. Roast under grill or in very hot oven, skin-side up, until skin blisters and blackens. Cover capsicum pieces with plastic or paper 5 minutes. Peel away and discard skin; slice capsicum flesh thickly.
5 Place capsicum and mesclun in large bowl with combined remaining ingredients. Divide salad among serving plates; top each with a baked ricotta.

serves 8
per serving 5.8g fat; 430kJ (103 cal)
tip Dried bay leaves and ¼ teaspoon crumbled dried sage can be substituted for the fresh varieties.

char-grilled polenta cakes

PREPARATION TIME 15 MINUTES (plus refrigeration time)   COOKING TIME 20 MINUTES

cooking-oil spray
1 litre (4 cups) water
1 teaspoon salt
1 cup (170g) polenta
2 tablespoons seeded mustard
2 trimmed corn cobs (500g)
1 medium red capsicum (200g),
   chopped finely
1 medium red onion (170g),
   chopped finely
1 lebanese cucumber (130g), seeded,
   chopped finely
¼ cup loosely packed, chopped
   fresh flat-leaf parsley
1 teaspoon finely grated lime rind
⅓ cup (80ml) lime juice
2 tablespoons olive oil
3 cloves garlic, crushed
1 tablespoon sweet chilli sauce

1 Lightly spray 23cm-square slab cake pan with cooking-oil spray. Bring the water and salt to a boil in large saucepan. Add polenta; cook, stirring, about 10 minutes or until polenta thickens. Add mustard; stir until combined. Spread polenta into slab pan. Cover; refrigerate about 30 minutes or until firm.
2 Meanwhile, boil, steam or microwave corn until just tender; drain. Cool; using sharp knife, remove kernels from cob. Combine corn in medium bowl with remaining ingredients.
3 Turn polenta onto board; cut into eight rectangles. Heat large lightly oiled non-stick frying pan; cook polenta, in batches, until browned both sides. Serve polenta cakes with corn salsa.

serves 8
per serving 6.3g fat; 753kJ (180 cal)
tip You can reduce preparation and cooking times by substituting the fresh corn for a 420g can of corn kernels, drained.

vietnamese spring rolls

PREPARATION TIME **1 HOUR** (plus standing time)
COOKING TIME **25 MINUTES** (plus cooling time)

1 medium red capsicum (200g)
1 medium carrot (120g)
1 tablespoon peanut oil
700g chicken breast fillets
1 tablespoon grated fresh ginger
2 cloves garlic, crushed
4 green onions, chopped finely
100g bean thread noodles
1 tablespoon chopped fresh vietnamese mint
500g bok choy, shredded finely
¼ cup (60ml) sweet chilli sauce
1 tablespoon soy sauce
40 spring roll wrappers
peanut oil, for deep-frying

DIPPING SAUCE
⅓ cup (80ml) sweet chilli sauce
2 tablespoons lime juice
3 green onions, chopped finely

1   Halve capsicum; discard seeds and membrane. Slice capsicum and carrot into paper-thin strips.
2   Heat half of the oil in medium saucepan; cook chicken, in batches, until browned and cooked through. Cool 10 minutes; shred finely.
3   Heat remaining oil in same pan; cook ginger, garlic and onion, stirring, about 2 minutes or until onion is soft.
4   Meanwhile, place noodles in large heatproof bowl. Cover with boiling water; stand 2 minutes. Drain noodles; chop coarsely.
5   Combine capsicum, carrot, chicken, onion mixture and noodles in large bowl with mint, bok choy and sauces.
6   Place a rounded tablespoon of the mixture across edge of one wrapper; roll to enclose filling, folding in ends. Place on tray, seam-side down. Repeat with remaining mixture and wrappers, placing on tray in single layer.
7   Just before serving, heat oil in wok or large deep-frying pan; deep-fry spring rolls, in batches, until golden brown and cooked through. Drain on absorbent paper; serve with dipping sauce.

dipping sauce   Combine ingredients in small bowl.

makes 40
per roll   4.3g fat; 307kJ (73 cal)
tips   Freeze spring rolls, in single layer, between sheets of plastic wrap. This makes it easier to remove and defrost small quantities at a time.
Frozen spring rolls can be deep-fried.
Use finely chopped fresh red thai chillies mixed with brown vinegar to make an alternative dipping sauce with more kick.

mediterranean grilled vegetables
with tomato vinaigrette

PREPARATION TIME 20 MINUTES (plus standing time)   COOKING TIME 1 HOUR

5 medium trimmed beetroot (825g)
2 medium eggplants (600g)
1 tablespoon salt
6 medium flat mushrooms (600g)
300g fetta cheese, crumbled
1/2 cup loosely packed fresh basil leaves

TOMATO VINAIGRETTE
4 large egg tomatoes (360g), halved
cooking-oil spray
1/4 cup (60ml) olive oil
2 tablespoons white wine vinegar
1 teaspoon salt

1 Preheat oven to hot.
2 Wrap beetroot individually in foil; place in baking dish. Bake in hot oven about 50 minutes or until tender; cool 5 minutes. Wearing gloves, peel while still warm; cut beetroot into 1cm slices.
3 Cut eggplant into 1cm slices; place in colander. Sprinkle with salt; stand 30 minutes. Rinse eggplant under cold running water; drain on absorbent paper.
4 Cook eggplant and mushrooms, in batches, on heated oiled grill plate (or grill or barbecue) until browned both sides.
5 Divide tomato vinaigrette among serving plates; top with mushroom, eggplant, beetroot, cheese and basil.

tomato vinaigrette Place tomato on oiled oven tray; coat with cooking-oil spray. Bake in hot oven about 40 minutes or until browned lightly. Blend or process tomato with oil, vinegar and salt until pureed. Push tomato vinaigrette through food mill or fine sieve into large bowl; discard pulp.

serves 6
per serving 22.5g fat; 1549kJ (371 cal)
tips Tomato vinaigrette can be made a day ahead and refrigerated, covered. You need approximately 1.5kg of untrimmed fresh beetroot for this recipe.

hot and sour soup

PREPARATION TIME 10 MINUTES   COOKING TIME 15 MINUTES

2cm piece galangal (10g),
  chopped coarsely
2 tablespoons coarsely chopped
  lemon grass
2 green onions, chopped coarsely
3 kaffir lime leaves
1 clove garlic, quartered
2 teaspoons peanut oil
1$\frac{1}{2}$ cups (375ml) vegetable stock
1.125 litres (4$\frac{1}{2}$ cups) water
2cm piece fresh ginger, sliced thinly
2 fresh red thai chillies, sliced thinly
425g can straw mushrooms,
  drained, rinsed
2 teaspoons sugar
$\frac{1}{3}$ cup (80ml) lime juice
2 teaspoons soy sauce
2 tablespoons coarsely chopped
  fresh coriander

1 Blend or process galangal, lemon grass, onion, lime leaves and garlic until chopped finely.
2 Heat oil in large saucepan; cook galangal mixture, stirring, until mixture is fragrant.
3 Add stock and the water; bring to a boil. Reduce heat; simmer, covered, 10 minutes. Strain stock mixture into large bowl; discard solids. Return stock mixture to same pan.
4 Return stock mixture to heat. Add ginger, chilli, mushrooms, sugar, juice and sauce; cook, uncovered, until hot. Just before serving, stir coriander through soup. Accompany soup with jasmine rice and wilted Asian greens, if desired.

serves 4
per serving 3g fat; 251kJ (60 cal)
tips For a milder flavour, remove seeds from the chillies.
The broth can be made ahead and frozen until required.

roast pumpkin, sesame and rocket salad

PREPARATION TIME **15 MINUTES** COOKING TIME **25 MINUTES**

600g trimmed pumpkin
cooking-oil spray
1 tablespoon honey
1 tablespoon sesame seeds
500g asparagus, halved
150g baby rocket leaves
1 small red onion (100g), sliced thinly
1 tablespoon sesame oil
1 tablespoon cider vinegar
1 teaspoon honey, extra

1 Preheat oven to very hot.
2 Cut pumpkin into 1.5cm wide strips.
3 Place pumpkin, in single layer, in baking dish lined with baking paper; spray lightly with cooking-oil spray. Roast, uncovered, in very hot oven about 20 minutes or until pumpkin is just tender. Drizzle with honey; sprinkle with seeds. Roast 5 minutes, uncovered, or until seeds are browned lightly.
4 Meanwhile, boil, steam or microwave asparagus until just tender; drain. Rinse under cold water; drain.
5 Combine pumpkin, asparagus, rocket and onion in large bowl. Drizzle with combined remaining ingredients; toss salad gently.

serves 6
per serving 5.3g fat; 505kJ (121 cal)
tips Reserve any seeds or honey from pumpkin pan and add to dressing. You will need a piece of pumpkin weighing approximately 750g for this recipe; we used butternut, but any variety can be used.

vine-ripened tomatoes and goat cheese in walnut dressing

PREPARATION TIME **15 MINUTES**

8 medium vine-ripened tomatoes (1.5kg), sliced thickly
150g goat cheese, sliced thickly
$1/4$ cup (25g) walnuts, toasted, chopped coarsely
$1/4$ cup (60ml) olive oil
1 clove garlic, crushed
$1^1/2$ tablespoons raspberry vinegar
2 teaspoons dijon mustard
2 teaspoons coarsely chopped fresh thyme
2 teaspoons sugar

1 Place a slice of tomato on each serving plate; top with a slice of cheese.
2 Repeat, sprinkling nuts and combined remaining ingredients between layers.

serves 6
per serving 18.5g fat; 938kJ (224 cal)
tips Hazelnuts can be substituted for walnuts in this recipe and, if you have hazelnut or walnut oil at hand, use one of these, rather than the olive oil.
Sample a few different goat cheeses before you decide on one; they vary greatly in texture and taste.

fresh rice paper rolls
with prawns

PREPARATION TIME 30 MINUTES   COOKING TIME 5 MINUTES (plus cooling time)

500g cooked medium prawns
1 cup (80g) finely shredded
  chinese cabbage
1/2 cup (120g) coarsely grated carrot
2 tablespoons coarsely chopped
  fresh mint
2 tablespoons coarsely chopped
  fresh coriander
12 small round dried rice paper
  wrappers (16cm)

DIPPING SAUCE
1/3 cup (75g) caster sugar
1/4 cup (60ml) white vinegar
1/4 cup (60ml) water
2 teaspoons fish sauce
2 fresh red thai chillies, sliced thinly
1 tablespoon chopped
  fresh coriander

1 Shell and devein prawns. Combine cabbage, carrot, mint and coriander in large bowl.

2 Place one sheet of rice paper in medium bowl of warm water until just softened. Remove from water; place on board. Place a tablespoon of the cabbage mixture in centre of rice paper; top with two prawns. Roll wrapper to enclose filling, folding in the ends. Repeat with remaining ingredients. Cover rolls with a damp towel to prevent rice paper from drying out.

3 Serve rolls with dipping sauce.

dipping sauce Place sugar, vinegar and the water in small saucepan; stir over medium heat until sugar dissolves. Bring to a boil; remove from heat. Stir in sauce and chilli; cool. Stir in coriander.

makes 12
per roll 0.3g fat; 220kJ (53 cal)
tip This recipe can be made 3 hours ahead.

prawns with chilli, coriander and lime butter

PREPARATION TIME **10 MINUTES**   COOKING TIME **5 MINUTES**

16 large uncooked king prawns
100g butter, melted
2 fresh red thai chillies, seeded, chopped finely
2 tablespoons lime juice
2 tablespoons finely chopped fresh coriander
50g mesclun

1   Shell prawns, leaving tails intact. To butterfly prawns, cut halfway through the back of each prawn. Remove veins; press flat.
2   Cook prawns on heated oiled grill pan or in heavy-base frying pan until changed in colour and just cooked through.
3   Meanwhile, combine butter, chilli, juice and coriander in medium bowl.
4   Serve mesclun with prawns, drizzled with hot butter mixture.

serves 4
per serving   21.2g fat; 1153kJ (275 cal)

roast tomatoes with garlic crumbs

PREPARATION TIME 5 MINUTES
COOKING TIME 25 MINUTES

**6 large egg tomatoes (540g),
   halved lengthways**

2 teaspoons balsamic vinegar

1 teaspoon caster sugar

1 teaspoon salt

1 tablespoon olive oil

1 clove garlic, crushed

½ cup (35g) stale breadcrumbs

1 tablespoon olive oil, extra

1 Preheat oven to hot.
2 Place tomato, cut-side up, in single layer on lightly
   greased oven tray. Brush tomato with vinegar; sprinkle
   with sugar and salt. Bake in hot oven about 20 minutes
   or until tender.
3 Heat oil in medium frying pan; cook garlic and
   breadcrumbs, stirring, about 5 minutes or until crumbs
   are golden brown. Remove from heat; drain on
   absorbent paper. Serve tomato, sprinkled with garlic
   crumbs and drizzled with extra oil.

serves 4
per serving 9.6g fat; 568kJ (136 cal)

roast vegetables with fetta

PREPARATION TIME 15 MINUTES
COOKING TIME 20 MINUTES

**4 baby eggplants (240g), sliced
   thinly lengthways**

1 large yellow capsicum (350g), sliced thickly

250g pumpkin, peeled, sliced thinly

2 tablespoons olive oil

2 tablespoons pine nuts, toasted

70g semi-dried tomatoes, drained

40g fetta cheese, crumbled

2 teaspoons balsamic vinegar

1 Preheat oven to very hot.
2 Combine eggplant, capsicum, pumpkin and oil in large
   baking dish. Cook vegetables in very hot oven about
   20 minutes or until tender. Add nuts and tomatoes.
   Serve vegetables sprinkled with fetta and vinegar.

serves 4
per serving 18.3g fat; 1032kJ (247 cal)

grilled oysters

PREPARATION TIME 5 MINUTES
COOKING TIME 10 MINUTES

40g butter, melted

$\frac{1}{3}$ cup (45g) finely chopped shaved ham

**2 tablespoons finely chopped fresh
flat-leaf parsley**

12 fresh oysters in half-shells

1 Combine butter, ham and parsley in small bowl.
Divide mixture evenly over oysters. Place oysters in
single layer on oven tray; cook under hot grill about
10 minutes or until ham is crisp.

serves 4
per serving 9.7g fat; 496kJ (119 cal)

prosciutto-wrapped haloumi

PREPARATION TIME 5 MINUTES
COOKING TIME 8 MINUTES

120g piece haloumi cheese

8 slices prosciutto

**2 tablespoons chopped fresh
flat-leaf parsley**

1 teaspoon lemon juice

1 Cut cheese into eight fingers. Wrap each finger in a
slice of prosciutto, securing ends with toothpicks.
Cook on heated oiled grill plate (or grill or barbecue)
about 8 minutes or until browned all over. Serve
sprinkled with parsley and juice.

serves 4
per serving 7.6g fat; 531kJ (127 cal)

fast

pasta & risotto

Pasta and rice are two of the easiest dishes to cook and they'll complement almost anything. Here are some delicious creations like pappardelle with chicken and creamy mushroom sauce, chilli prawn linguine, and risotto primavera.

chilli prawn linguine

PREPARATION TIME **15 MINUTES**   COOKING TIME **15 MINUTES**

500g linguine
⅓ cup (80ml) olive oil
400g royal red prawns
3 fresh red thai chillies, seeded,
  chopped finely
2 cloves garlic, crushed
½ cup chopped fresh flat-leaf parsley
2 teaspoons finely grated lemon rind

1 Cook pasta in large saucepan of boiling water, uncovered, until just tender; drain.
2 Meanwhile, heat oil in large frying pan; cook prawns, chilli and garlic, stirring, until prawns are just cooked through.
3 Remove from heat; stir in parsley and rind.
4 Combine pasta with prawn mixture in large bowl; toss gently.

serves 4
per serving 20.5g fat; 2795kJ (669 cal)
tips Royal red prawns are peeled, uncooked pink prawns. They will be opaque when cooked.
This recipe is best made just before serving.
Spaghetti can be substituted for the linguine.

spaghetti with mussels and clams

PREPARATION TIME 20 MINUTES   COOKING TIME 15 MINUTES

500g mussels
500g clams
¹/₄ cup (60ml) dry white wine
¹/₄ cup (60ml) water
500g spaghetti
¹/₃ cup (80ml) extra virgin olive oil
2 cloves garlic, crushed
1 fresh red thai chilli, chopped finely
2 medium tomatoes (380g), seeded,
  chopped coarsely
¹/₂ cup chopped fresh flat-leaf parsley

1   Scrub mussels; remove beards. Rinse clams.
2   Combine wine and the water in large saucepan; bring to a boil. Add mussels and clams; reduce heat. Simmer, covered, until shells open; discard any that do not open. Cover seafood to keep warm. Strain cooking liquid through fine sieve into medium jug; reserve ¹/₃ cup (80ml) of the liquid.
3   Cook pasta in large saucepan of boiling water until tender; drain. Return to pan.
4   Meanwhile, heat oil in large frying pan; cook garlic and chilli, stirring, until fragrant. Add tomatoes and reserved cooking liquid; simmer, uncovered, until hot.
5   Add seafood to pasta with oil mixture and parsley; toss gently.

serves 6
per serving 13.5g fat; 1814kJ (433 cal)
tip This recipe is best made just before serving.

ricotta and capsicum ravioli with rocket dressing

PREPARATION TIME **40 MINUTES**   COOKING TIME **30 MINUTES**

3 large red capsicums (1kg)
2 green onions, chopped finely
1 clove garlic, crushed
2$\frac{1}{2}$ cups (500g) ricotta cheese
72 wonton wrappers
300g baby rocket leaves
$\frac{1}{2}$ cup (125ml) olive oil
2 tablespoons lemon juice
2 tablespoons balsamic vinegar
2 teaspoons sugar
1 clove garlic, quartered, extra
$\frac{1}{4}$ cup (20g) shaved parmesan cheese

1   Quarter capsicums; remove and discard seeds and membrane. Roast under grill or in very hot oven, skin-side up, until skin blisters and blackens. Cover capsicum quarters in plastic or paper 5 minutes. Peel away and discard skin; chop capsicum flesh finely.

2   Combine capsicum, onion, garlic and ricotta in medium bowl.

3   Place a level tablespoon of the capsicum filling in the centre of 36 wonton wrappers; brush edges lightly with a little water. Top each with remaining wonton wrappers; press edges together to seal the ravioli.

4   Reserve approximately a fifth of the rocket. Blend or process remaining rocket, oil, juice, vinegar, sugar and extra garlic until pureed. Strain into medium jug; discard pulp.

5   Cook ravioli, in batches, in large saucepan of boiling water, uncovered, until tender; drain. Serve ravioli drizzled with rocket dressing; top with reserved rocket and parmesan.

serves 6
per serving 30.9g fat; 1913kJ (458 cal)
tip Make the ravioli a day ahead and refrigerate, on a covered tray, until just before you want to cook them.

risotto primavera

PREPARATION TIME **10 MINUTES**   COOKING TIME **25 MINUTES**

20g butter
2 teaspoons olive oil
1 medium leek (350g), sliced thinly
1 clove garlic, crushed
2 cups (400g) arborio rice
³/₄ cup (180ml) dry white wine
1¹/₂ cups (375ml) vegetable stock
2¹/₂ cups (625ml) water
150g sugar snap peas
300g asparagus, sliced thickly
100g yellow patty-pan
   squash, quartered
²/₃ cup (50g) finely grated
   parmesan cheese
¹/₃ cup (80ml) cream

1 Heat butter and oil in large saucepan; cook leek and garlic, stirring, until leek softens.
2 Add rice, wine, stock and the water; bring to a boil. Reduce heat; simmer, covered, 15 minutes, stirring occasionally.
3 Stir in peas, asparagus and squash; cook, covered, about 5 minutes or until rice is just tender.
4 Just before serving, stir in cheese and cream.

serves 4
per serving 20.4g fat; 2632kJ (630 cal)
tip Medium-grain rice can be used instead of arborio.

farfalle with baked salmon, caperberries and dill

PREPARATION TIME **25 MINUTES**   COOKING TIME **30 MINUTES**

2 large red onions (600g)
1 cup (160g) caperberries,
   rinsed, drained
cooking-oil spray
1 fresh red thai chilli, seeded,
   chopped finely
¹/₄ cup loosely packed, finely
   chopped fresh dill
2 teaspoons olive oil
1kg piece skinless salmon fillet
500g farfalle
²/₃ cup (160ml) dry white wine
2 tablespoons lemon juice
¹/₂ cup (125ml) light cream
250g baby rocket leaves, trimmed

1 Preheat oven to moderately hot.

2 Cut each onion into eight wedges; place, in single layer, in large baking dish with caperberries. Spray lightly with cooking-oil spray; roast, uncovered, in moderately hot oven about 25 minutes or until onion is just softened.

3 Meanwhile, combine chilli and half of the dill in small bowl with olive oil. Place salmon on large baking-paper lined oven tray; brush salmon both sides with chilli mixture. Roast, uncovered, in moderately hot oven about 10 minutes or until salmon is just tender and cooked as desired.

4 Cook pasta, uncovered, in large saucepan of boiling water until just tender. While pasta is cooking, combine wine and juice in small saucepan; bring to a boil. Reduce heat; simmer, uncovered, about 5 minutes or until liquid reduces by half. Add cream and remaining dill.

5 Place pasta, flaked salmon, onion mixture and dill cream sauce in large bowl with baby rocket leaves; toss gently to combine.

serves 8
per serving 15g fat; 2090kJ (500 cal)

leek and asparagus risotto

PREPARATION TIME **15 MINUTES**   COOKING TIME **45 MINUTES**

1$^1\!/_2$ cups (375ml) dry white wine
1.5 litres (6 cups) chicken stock
1 tablespoon olive oil
2 medium leeks (700g), sliced thinly
2 cloves garlic, crushed
3 cups (600g) arborio rice
500g asparagus, trimmed, chopped coarsely
$^1\!/_3$ cup (25g) finely grated parmesan cheese
1 tablespoon shredded fresh basil

1 Combine wine and stock in large saucepan; bring to a boil. Reduce heat; simmer, covered, to keep hot.
2 Meanwhile, heat oil in large saucepan; cook leek and garlic, stirring, until leek softens.
3 Add rice; stir to coat in leek mixture. Stir in 1 cup (250ml) of the hot stock mixture; cook, stirring, over low heat until liquid is absorbed. Continue adding stock mixture, in 1-cup batches, stirring, until liquid is absorbed after each addition. Total cooking time should be about 30 minutes or until rice is just tender.
4 Add asparagus; cook, stirring, until asparagus is just tender. Just before serving, stir in cheese. Serve sprinkled with basil.

serves 8
per serving 4.7g fat; 1550kJ (371 cal)
tip Fresh sugar snap peas can be substituted for the asparagus.

fettuccini with rocket pesto and fresh tomato salsa

PREPARATION TIME **10 MINUTES**   COOKING TIME **15 MINUTES**

500g fettuccine
8 cloves garlic, quartered
$^{1}/_{2}$ cup loosely packed, chopped fresh basil
120g rocket, chopped coarsely
$^{2}/_{3}$ cup (160ml) olive oil
$^{1}/_{2}$ cup (40g) finely grated parmesan cheese
3 medium tomatoes (570g), chopped coarsely
2 tablespoons lemon juice
2 fresh red thai chillies, sliced thinly
$^{1}/_{3}$ cup (50g) pine nuts, toasted

1 Cook pasta in large saucepan of boiling water, uncovered, until just tender; drain.
2 Meanwhile, blend or process garlic, basil, rocket and oil until smooth.
3 Combine pasta, rocket pesto, cheese, tomato, juice and chilli in large saucepan; cook, stirring, until hot. Add nuts; toss gently to combine.

serves 4
per serving 50.3g fat; 3780kJ (904 cal)
tip You could substitute baby spinach leaves for the rocket to give a milder-flavoured pesto.

pappardelle with chicken and creamy mushroom sauce

PREPARATION TIME 15 MINUTES   COOKING TIME 12 MINUTES

2 tablespoons olive oil
1 clove garlic, crushed
1 small onion (80g), chopped finely
250g swiss brown mushrooms, sliced thinly
1 cup (250ml) cream
2 teaspoons finely chopped fresh rosemary
50g butter, chopped
500g pappardelle
200g cooked chicken, shredded thinly
$^1/_2$ cup (50g) walnut pieces, toasted
$^3/_4$ cup (60g) finely grated parmesan cheese
$^1/_4$ cup chopped fresh flat-leaf parsley

1   Heat oil in large frying pan; cook garlic and onion, stirring, until onion softens. Add mushroom; cook, stirring, until tender.

2   Add cream and rosemary to pan. Bring to a boil; reduce heat. Simmer, uncovered, about 3 minutes or until sauce thickens; stir in butter.

3   Meanwhile, cook pasta in large saucepan of boiling water, uncovered, until just tender. Drain pasta; return to pan.

4   Add hot cream sauce to hot pasta with chicken, nuts, half of the cheese, and parsley; toss gently until combined.

5   Serve immediately, topped with remaining cheese.

serves 6
per serving 44g fat; 3078kJ (735 cal)
tip This recipe is best made just before serving.

roasted capsicum, goat cheese and walnut salad

PREPARATION TIME **10 MINUTES**   COOKING TIME **20 MINUTES**

375g large spiral pasta
2 medium red capsicums (400g)
2 medium yellow capsicums (400g)
150g goat cheese, crumbled
$1/3$ cup (35g) walnuts, toasted, chopped coarsely
$1/2$ cup loosely packed fresh basil leaves
$1/4$ cup (60ml) red wine vinegar
$1/3$ cup (80ml) olive oil
1 clove garlic, crushed
2 teaspoons seeded mustard

1   Cook pasta in large saucepan of boiling water, uncovered, until just tender; drain. Rinse under cold water; drain.
2   Meanwhile, quarter capsicums; remove and discard seeds and membranes. Roast under grill or in very hot oven, skin-side up, until skin blisters and blackens. Cover capsicum pieces with plastic or paper 5 minutes. Peel away and discard skin; slice capsicum flesh thickly.
3   Place pasta and capsicum in large bowl with cheese, nuts, basil and combined remaining ingredients; toss gently to combine.

serves 4
per serving 31.5g fat; 2703kJ (647 cal)
tip Fetta or any soft, crumbly cheese can be substituted for the goat cheese, and toasted pecan halves can be used instead of walnuts.

mushroom risotto

PREPARATION TIME **15 MINUTES** COOKING TIME **45 MINUTES**

1 cup (250ml) olive oil
2 tablespoons fresh sage leaves
500g mixed mushrooms, sliced thinly
3 cloves garlic, crushed
60g butter, chopped
2 medium brown onions (300g),
   chopped finely
2 cups (400g) arborio rice
1.5 litres (6 cups) vegetable stock
$^{1}/_{2}$ cup (40g) finely grated
   parmesan cheese

1 Heat oil in small saucepan; carefully cook a few of the sage leaves until bright green. Remove from pan with slotted spoon; drain on absorbent paper. Repeat with remaining sage leaves; reserve.

2 Transfer 2 tablespoons of the oil to large saucepan; cook mushroom, stirring, until browned and just tender. Add garlic; stir until fragrant. Remove mushroom mixture from pan; reserve.

3 Heat half of the butter in same pan; cook onion, stirring, over low heat until soft but not coloured. Add rice; stir until rice is coated in butter mixture.

4 Meanwhile, bring stock to a boil in large saucepan. Reduce heat; simmer. Add 1 cup (250ml) of the stock to rice mixture; cook, stirring, over low heat until liquid is absorbed. Continue adding stock, in 1-cup batches, stirring, until liquid is absorbed after each addition. Total cooking time should be about 30 minutes or until rice is just tender.

5 Stir in cheese, remaining butter and reserved mushroom mixture. Risotto should be creamy; add a little boiling water, if necessary, and serve topped with reserved sage leaves.

serves 6
per serving 21.2g fat; 2017kJ (412 cal)
tip Mushroom can be cooked 3 hours ahead. The risotto is best made just before serving.

baked pumpkin and spinach risotto

PREPARATION TIME **15 MINUTES**   COOKING TIME **35 MINUTES**

**500g butternut pumpkin,
    chopped coarsely**
2 tablespoons olive oil
1½ cups (375ml) chicken stock
1.25 litres (5 cups) water
**1 large brown onion (200g),
    chopped coarsely**
2 cloves garlic, crushed
2 cups (400g) arborio rice
½ cup (125ml) dry white wine
**500g english spinach, trimmed,
    chopped coarsely**
½ cup (80g) pine nuts, toasted
½ cup (40g) grated parmesan cheese
½ cup (125ml) cream

1   Preheat oven to hot. Combine pumpkin with half of the oil in baking dish. Bake, uncovered, in hot oven about 20 minutes or until tender; reserve.
2   Meanwhile, combine stock and the water in large saucepan; bring to a boil. Reduce heat; simmer.
3   Heat remaining oil in large saucepan; cook onion and garlic, stirring, until onion is soft. Add rice; stir to coat in oil mixture. Add wine; stir until almost evaporated.
4   Stir in 1 cup (250ml) of the hot stock mixture; cook, stirring, over low heat until liquid is absorbed. Continue adding stock mixture, in 1-cup batches, stirring, until liquid is absorbed after each addition. Total cooking time should be about 30 minutes or until rice is just tender.
5   Add spinach, pine nuts, cheese and cream; cook, stirring, until spinach wilts. Gently stir in reserved baked pumpkin.
6   Serve topped with parmesan cheese flakes, if desired.

serves 4
per serving   41.6g fat; 3504kJ (837 cal)
tip   Pumpkin can be baked 3 hours ahead. The risotto is best made just before serving.

pasta with fresh tomato sauce

PREPARATION TIME **15 MINUTES**   COOKING TIME **5 MINUTES**

375g fresh lasagne sheets, sliced thickly
2 tablespoons extra virgin olive oil
6 medium tomatoes (1.2kg), peeled, seeded, chopped coarsely
¼ cup loosely packed, chopped fresh basil
2 cloves garlic, crushed
2 teaspoons red wine vinegar
1 fresh red thai chilli, seeded, chopped finely
80g low-fat fetta cheese, crumbled

1 Cook pasta in large saucepan of boiling water, uncovered, until just tender; drain. Sprinkle half of the oil over pasta; toss gently to combine.
2 Combine tomato, basil, garlic, remaining oil, vinegar and chilli in medium bowl.
3 Divide pasta among serving plates. Spoon tomato mixture over pasta; sprinkle with cheese.

serves 8
per serving 6.3g fat; 535kJ (128 cal)
tip To peel tomatoes, slice a cross in the bottom of each tomato. Place tomatoes in large bowl of boiling water 1 minute; drain. Rinse under cold running water; peel.

meat

Tandoori lamb cutlets, beef and vegetables with herb pesto, mustard veal with polenta and spinach puree, and spicy pork ribs are a few of the creative lamb, beef, veal and pork recipes for you to try.

mustard veal with polenta and spinach puree

PREPARATION TIME **15 MINUTES** COOKING TIME **20 MINUTES**

¹/₃ **cup (95g) seeded mustard**
2 tablespoons coarsely chopped
   fresh oregano
2 cloves garlic, crushed
4 veal chops (600g)
4 large egg tomatoes (360g), halved
2 cups (500ml) water
1 teaspoon salt
1 cup (170g) polenta
³/₄ **cup (180ml) skim milk**
¹/₄ **cup (20g) finely grated**
   parmesan cheese
2kg spinach, trimmed
2 cloves garlic, crushed, extra
2 anchovy fillets, drained
2 tablespoons lemon juice
¹/₄ **cup (60ml) beef stock**

1 Combine mustard, oregano and garlic in small bowl; brush both sides of veal with mustard mixture.
2 Cook veal and tomato, in batches, on heated lightly oiled grill plate (or grill or barbecue) until veal is browned both sides and cooked as desired and tomato is browned and tender.
3 Meanwhile, bring combined water and salt to a boil in medium saucepan. Stir in polenta; cook, stirring, about 10 minutes or until polenta thickens. Stir in milk; cook, stirring, about 5 minutes or until polenta thickens. Stir in cheese.
4 Boil, steam or microwave spinach until just wilted; squeeze out excess liquid with hands. Blend or process spinach with remaining ingredients until pureed.
5 Serve veal chops with tomato, polenta and spinach puree.

serves 4
per serving 7.3g fat; 1626kJ (389 cal)
tip Fresh rosemary or thyme can be substituted for the oregano.

lamb kofta with chilli and yogurt sauce

PREPARATION TIME **20 MINUTES**   COOKING TIME **10 MINUTES**

1kg lean lamb mince
1 large brown onion (200g),
    chopped finely
1 clove garlic, crushed
1 tablespoon ground cumin
2 teaspoons ground turmeric
2 teaspoons ground allspice
1 tablespoon finely chopped
    fresh mint
2 tablespoons chopped fresh
    flat-leaf parsley
1 egg, beaten lightly
6 pocket pitta, quartered

YOGURT SAUCE
$^3/_4$ cup (200g) low-fat yogurt
1 clove garlic, crushed
1 tablespoon chopped fresh
    flat-leaf parsley

CHILLI TOMATO SAUCE
$^1/_4$ cup (60ml) tomato sauce
$^1/_4$ cup (60ml) chilli sauce

1 Using hands, combine lamb, onion, garlic, spices, herbs and egg in large bowl; shape mixture into 18 balls. Mould balls around skewers to form sausage shapes. Cook, in batches, on heated oiled grill plate (or grill or barbecue) until browned all over and cooked through.

2 Serve kofta with pitta, yogurt sauce and chilli tomato sauce. Serve with tabbouleh, if desired.

yogurt sauce Combine ingredients in small bowl.
chilli tomato sauce Combine sauces in small bowl.

serves 6
per serving 14.5g fat; 1817kJ (435 cal)
tips You will need 18 bamboo skewers for this recipe. Soak skewers in water for at least an hour before use, to prevent them from splintering or scorching.
Kofta can be finger-, ball- or torpedo-shaped but all are made of minced meat and spices, then hand-moulded before grilling.

beef and rice noodle stir-fry

PREPARATION TIME **15 MINUTES**   COOKING TIME **20 MINUTES**

500g fresh rice noodles
2 tablespoons peanut oil
500g beef fillets, sliced thinly
1 clove garlic, crushed
1 tablespoon grated fresh ginger
1 tablespoon finely chopped fresh lemon grass
1 fresh red thai chilli, seeded, chopped finely
1 tablespoon chopped fresh mint
1 large carrot (180g), halved lengthways, sliced thinly
200g fresh baby corn, halved lengthways
200g chinese broccoli, chopped coarsely
1 tablespoon brown sugar
2 teaspoons cornflour
¼ cup (60ml) rice wine
¼ cup (60ml) oyster sauce
2 tablespoons light soy sauce

1 Rinse noodles under hot water; drain. Transfer to large bowl; separate noodles with fork.
2 Heat half of the oil in wok or large frying pan; stir-fry beef, in batches, until browned all over.
3 Heat remaining oil in wok; stir-fry garlic, ginger, lemon grass, chilli and mint until fragrant. Add carrot and corn; stir-fry until carrot is just tender.
4 Return beef to wok with broccoli, sugar and blended cornflour, wine and sauces; stir-fry until broccoli just wilts and sauce boils and thickens slightly. Add noodles; stir-fry until hot.

serves 4
per serving 16.5g fat; 2011kJ (481 cal)
tip Fresh rice noodles must be rinsed under hot water to remove starch and excess oil before using. You can substitute egg noodles for the rice noodles.

chilli pork with oyster sauce

PREPARATION TIME **15 MINUTES**   COOKING TIME **10 MINUTES**

1 tablespoon peanut oil
450g pork fillets, sliced thinly
1 clove garlic, crushed
1 medium white onion (150g), sliced thinly
1 large red capsicum (350g), sliced thinly
1 small green zucchini (90g), sliced thinly
1 small yellow zucchini (90g), sliced thinly
¹/₄ cup (60ml) oyster sauce
1 tablespoon mild sweet chilli sauce
1 tablespoon chopped fresh coriander

1 Heat oil in wok or large frying pan. Stir-fry pork, in batches, until browned.
2 Stir-fry garlic and onion until onion is just soft.
3 Add capsicum and zucchini; stir-fry.
4 Return pork to wok. Add sauces; stir-fry until hot. Serve sprinkled with coriander.

serves 4
per serving 7.6g fat; 907kJ (217 cal)

beef and vegetables with herb pesto

PREPARATION TIME 25 MINUTES   COOKING TIME 15 MINUTES

1 tablespoon olive oil
400g beef steak, sliced thinly
1 clove garlic, crushed
20 baby carrots, halved lengthways
1 medium red capsicum (200g), chopped coarsely
1 medium yellow capsicum (200g), chopped coarsely
200g sugar snap peas
$^1/_2$ cup (125ml) beef stock

HERB PESTO
1$^1/_2$ cups firmly packed fresh basil leaves
$^1/_4$ cup firmly packed fresh oregano leaves
$^1/_3$ cup (25g) grated parmesan cheese
$^1/_4$ cup (60ml) olive oil
$^1/_4$ cup (60ml) cream
1 clove garlic, crushed
1 tablespoon balsamic vinegar
2 teaspoons water

1 Heat oil in wok or large frying pan. Stir-fry beef and garlic, in batches, until beef is browned.
2 Stir-fry carrot and capsicum.
3 Return beef mixture to wok with peas and stock; stir until hot.
4 Serve stir-fry topped with warm herb pesto.

herb pesto Blend or process herbs, cheese, oil, cream, garlic, vinegar and the water until combined. Transfer mixture to small saucepan; stir over low heat, without boiling, until heated through.

serves 4
per serving 31.9g fat; 1893kJ (453 cal)

spicy pork ribs

PREPARATION TIME **10 MINUTES**   COOKING TIME **20 MINUTES**

1.5kg trimmed pork spare rib slabs
³/₄ cup (180ml) light soy sauce
1 egg, beaten lightly
¹/₄ cup (35g) plain flour
2 tablespoons vegetable oil
¹/₂ cup (125ml) rice wine
¹/₂ cup (100g) firmly packed brown sugar
¹/₄ cup (50g) yellow mustard seeds
¹/₃ cup loosely packed, chopped fresh coriander
3 cloves garlic, crushed
1 tablespoon grated fresh ginger
3 teaspoons dried chilli flakes
1 teaspoon five-spice powder
¹/₂ teaspoon cayenne pepper

1 Cut pork into individual-rib pieces.
2 Place ribs in large saucepan. Cover with water; bring to a boil. Reduce heat; simmer, uncovered, about 10 minutes or until ribs are almost cooked through. Drain; pat dry with absorbent paper.
3 Blend ¼ cup (60ml) of the soy sauce with the egg and flour in large bowl. Add ribs; stir to coat in soy mixture.
4 Heat oil in wok or large frying pan; stir-fry ribs, in batches, until browned all over.
5 Cook remaining soy sauce and remaining ingredients in wok, stirring, until sugar dissolves. Return ribs to wok; stir-fry until heated through. Serve with steamed rice and individual finger bowls filled with water and a few slices of lemon, if desired.

serves 4
per serving 17.7g fat; 2066kJ (494 cal)
tips Spicy spare ribs can be made a day ahead and refrigerated, covered, or frozen for up to 3 months. To serve, reheat in the microwave oven or wok.
Ask your butcher to cut the pork ribs "American-style" so that as much fat as possible has been removed, leaving only tender, flavoursome meat.

pork fillet with apple and leek

PREPARATION TIME 10 MINUTES (plus standing time)   COOKING TIME 25 MINUTES

800g pork fillets
³/₄ cup (180ml) chicken stock
2 medium leeks (700g), sliced thickly
1 clove garlic, crushed
2 tablespoons brown sugar
2 tablespoons red wine vinegar
2 medium apples (300g)
10g butter
1 tablespoon brown sugar, extra
400g baby carrots, trimmed, halved
8 medium patty-pan squash
  (100g), quartered
250g asparagus, trimmed,
  chopped coarsely

1 Preheat oven to very hot.
2 Place pork, in single layer, in large baking dish; bake, uncovered, in very hot oven about 25 minutes or until pork is browned and cooked as desired. Cover; stand 5 minutes before slicing thickly.
3 Meanwhile, heat half of the stock in medium frying pan; cook leek and garlic, stirring, until leek softens and browns slightly. Add sugar and vinegar; cook, stirring, about 5 minutes or until leek caramelises. Add remaining stock; bring to a boil. Reduce heat; simmer, uncovered, about 5 minutes or until liquid reduces by half. Place leek mixture in medium bowl; cover to keep warm.
4 Peel, core and halve apples; cut into thick slices.
5 Melt butter in same pan as used for leek mixture; cook apple and extra sugar, stirring, until apple is browned and tender.
6 Boil, steam or microwave carrot, squash and asparagus, separately, until just tender; drain.
7 Serve pork, topped with caramelised apple and sweet and sour leek, on top of the mixed vegetables.

serves 4
per serving 7.5g fat; 1624kJ (389 cal)
tip You can make the sweet and sour leek 3 hours ahead; reheat before serving.

tandoori lamb cutlets

PREPARATION TIME 20 MINUTES   COOKING TIME 10 MINUTES

12 lamb cutlets (900g)
$^1/_2$ cup (150g) tandoori paste
$^3/_4$ cup (200g) yogurt

CHUTNEY
1 tablespoon vegetable oil
1 small red onion (100g), chopped finely
2 large tomatoes (500g), chopped finely
1 tablespoon lime juice
1 tablespoon sweet chilli sauce
2 tablespoons chopped fresh coriander

RAITA
1 lebanese cucumber (130g), seeded,
  chopped finely
2 tablespoons finely chopped fresh mint
$^3/_4$ cup (200g) yogurt

1 Combine lamb with paste and yogurt in large bowl.
2 Cook lamb on heated oiled grill plate (or grill or barbecue), in batches, until browned both sides and cooked as desired.
3 Serve lamb with separate bowls of chutney and raita. Top with thinly sliced green onion, if desired.

chutney Combine ingredients in small bowl.
raita Combine ingredients in small bowl.

serves 4
per serving 49.4g fat; 2553kJ (611 cal)
tip Lamb can be marinated a day ahead and refrigerated, covered.

teriyaki beef stir-fry

PREPARATION TIME **15 MINUTES**   COOKING TIME **20 MINUTES**

2 tablespoons peanut oil
2 teaspoons sesame oil
2 cloves garlic, sliced thinly
600g piece beef rump steak, sliced thinly
1 medium brown onion (150g), sliced thickly
230g can bamboo shoots, drained
$\frac{1}{2}$ cup (40g) bean sprouts
$\frac{1}{4}$ cup (60ml) teriyaki sauce
$\frac{1}{3}$ cup (80ml) beef stock
450g hokkien noodles
4 green onions, sliced thickly

1   Heat oils in wok or large non-stick frying pan; stir-fry garlic and
    beef, in batches, until beef is browned.
2   Stir-fry brown onion and bamboo shoots 2 minutes.
3   Return beef mixture to wok with sprouts. Stir in sauce and stock;
    stir-fry until mixture boils.
4   Meanwhile, place noodles in medium heatproof bowl; cover with
    boiling water, separate with fork, drain. Serve stir-fry with noodles;
    sprinkle with green onion.

serves 4
per serving   20g fat; 2643kJ (632 cal)
tip   Recipe best made just before serving.

pepper steak with scalloped potatoes

PREPARATION TIME **15 MINUTES** COOKING TIME **55 MINUTES**

6 beef fillet steaks (600g)
2 teaspoons freshly ground
  black pepper
1 clove garlic, crushed
1 tablespoon cornflour
1 cup (250ml) beef stock

SCALLOPED POTATOES
2 medium brown onions (300g),
  sliced thinly
2 cloves garlic, crushed
5 medium potatoes (1kg),
  sliced thinly
$^1/_2$ cup (120g) light sour cream
$^1/_2$ cup (125ml) chicken stock
1 cup (125g) coarsely grated low-fat
  cheddar cheese

1 Prepare scalloped potatoes.
2 Coat beef all over with pepper; cook, in batches, in large heated lightly oiled non-stick frying pan until browned both sides and cooked as desired. Cover beef to keep warm.
3 Cook garlic in same pan, stirring, until fragrant. Blend cornflour with stock in small jug; add to pan. Stir over heat until sauce mixture boils and thickens slightly. Drizzle steaks with sauce; serve with scalloped potatoes.

scalloped potatoes Preheat oven to moderate. Heat large lightly oiled non-stick frying pan. Cook onion and garlic, stirring, until onion softens. Layer onion mixture and potato in shallow 2.5-litre (10-cup) baking dish, finishing with potato layer. Pour combined sour cream and stock over potato mixture; sprinkle with cheese. Bake, covered, in moderate oven 45 minutes. Uncover; bake further 10 minutes or until tender and browned lightly on top.

serves 6
per serving 10.5g fat; 1124kJ (269 cal)

gingered pork with vegetables

PREPARATION TIME **10 MINUTES** (plus marinating time)   COOKING TIME **15 MINUTES**

700g pork fillets, sliced thinly
2 tablespoons grated fresh ginger
¼ cup chopped fresh coriander
2 tablespoons rice vinegar
2 tablespoons peanut oil
125g fresh baby corn,
   halved lengthways
1 medium red capsicum (200g),
   sliced thinly
100g snow peas, halved
2 tablespoons light soy sauce
250g spinach, trimmed
3 cups (240g) bean sprouts
½ cup fresh coriander leaves, extra

1 Combine pork in medium bowl with ginger, coriander and vinegar. Cover; marinate in refrigerator 3 hours or overnight.
2 Heat half of the oil in wok or large frying pan; stir-fry pork mixture, in batches, until pork is browned and cooked through.
3 Heat remaining oil in same wok. Stir-fry corn, capsicum and peas until just tender; remove from wok. Return pork to wok with soy sauce; stir-fry until heated through. Just before serving, return cooked vegetables to wok and gently toss with pork, spinach, sprouts and extra coriander until spinach just wilts.

serves 4
per serving 13.8g fat; 1443kJ (345 cal)

lamb cutlets with potato and parsnip mash

PREPARATION TIME **15 MINUTES (plus marinating time)**
COOKING TIME **20 MINUTES**

18 french-trimmed lamb cutlets (1.4kg)
4 cloves garlic, crushed
2 teaspoons grated fresh ginger
1/4 cup chopped fresh mint
1/3 cup (80ml) balsamic vinegar
2 large potatoes (600g), chopped coarsely
5 medium parsnips (625g), chopped coarsely
1/2 cup (125ml) buttermilk
1 1/2 cups (375ml) vegetable stock

1   Combine lamb in large bowl with garlic, ginger, mint and half of the vinegar; toss to coat lamb all over. Cover; marinate in refrigerator 3 hours or overnight.
2   Boil, steam or microwave potato and parsnip until tender; drain. Mash potato and parsnip in large bowl with buttermilk until smooth.
3   Meanwhile, heat large lightly oiled non-stick frying pan; cook lamb, in batches, until browned both sides and cooked as desired. Cover to keep warm.
4   Add remaining vinegar and stock to same pan; bring to a boil. Reduce heat; simmer, uncovered, until sauce reduces by two-thirds. Serve lamb with mash; drizzle with strained sauce.

serves 6
per serving 11.8g fat; 1396kJ (334 cal)

mushroom pizza

PREPARATION TIME 10 MINUTES
COOKING TIME 15 MINUTES

4 x 15cm pizza bases
1½ cups (185g) grated pizza cheese
150g flat mushrooms, sliced thinly
100g fetta cheese, crumbled
2 tablespoons finely chopped fresh chives

1 Preheat oven to hot. Place pizza bases on oven tray. Sprinkle half the pizza cheese over bases. Divide mushroom, fetta cheese, chives and remaining pizza cheese among bases.
2 Bake, uncovered, in hot oven about 15 minutes or until pizza tops are browned lightly and bases are crisp.

serves 4
per serving 22.1g fat; 2325kJ (556 cal)
tips We used a Greek fetta, which crumbles well and has a sharp taste, for this recipe.
Any fresh or frozen pizza bases would be suitable.

greek wrap

PREPARATION TIME 10 MINUTES

80g baby spinach leaves
140g fetta cheese, crumbled
2½ cups (425g) coarsely chopped cooked chicken
200g tzatziki
4 pieces lavash bread

1 Combine spinach, cheese, chicken and tzatziki in large bowl.
2 Place a quarter of the mixture along short side of one piece of lavash; roll to enclose filling. Repeat with remaining mixture and bread. Use toothpicks to secure wraps, if necessary.

serves 4
per serving 20.5g fat; 1940kJ (464 cal)
tip Wrap can be made 2 hours ahead and refrigerated, covered tightly with plastic wrap.

lamb pide

PREPARATION TIME 10 MINUTES
COOKING TIME 20 MINUTES

2 small brown onions (160g), chopped finely

2 cloves garlic, crushed

250g lamb mince

1 tablespoon tomato paste

¼ teaspoon hot paprika

1 teaspoon ground cumin

2 small pide

¼ cup (25g) finely grated low-fat mozzarella cheese

2 tablespoons chopped fresh mint

1 Preheat oven to hot.
2 Cook onion and garlic in lightly oiled medium saucepan, stirring, until onion softens. Add lamb, paste, paprika and cumin; cook, stirring, until lamb is cooked through.
3 Split bread; place bases on oven tray. Spread with lamb mixture; sprinkle with cheese and mint. Replace tops; bake, uncovered, in hot oven about 10 minutes or until bread is crisp.

serves 4
per serving 8.6g fat; 1549kJ (371 cal)

salami and rocket pizza

PREPARATION TIME 10 MINUTES
COOKING TIME 15 MINUTES

2 x 26cm pizza bases

²⁄₃ cup (160ml) tomato pasta sauce

250g mozzarella cheese, sliced thinly

125g salami, sliced thinly

50g baby rocket leaves

1 Preheat oven to hot.
2 Place pizza bases on oven trays. Spread sauce evenly over bases; top with cheese and salami. Bake, uncovered, in hot oven about 15 minutes or until cheese melts and bases are crisp.
3 Just before serving, top pizzas with rocket and freshly ground pepper, if desired.

serves 4
per serving 30.3g fat; 2818kJ (673 cal)
tips Pizza is best made just before serving. Any fresh or frozen pizza bases would be suitable.

seafood

Hot and spicy fish cutlets, prawn laksa,
and smoked salmon and caviar salad
are all perfect to serve as a casual summer
lunch or a lovely light evening meal.

fish with garlic and chilli

PREPARATION TIME **5 MINUTES**   COOKING TIME **8 MINUTES**

¹/₄ cup (60ml) olive oil
4 blue eye fish fillets with
**   skin on (800g)**
1 clove garlic, crushed
1¹/₂ tablespoons sherry vinegar
1 teaspoon dried chilli flakes
2 tablespoons chopped fresh
**   flat-leaf parsley**

1   Heat 1 tablespoon of the oil in large non-stick frying pan. Cook fish, flesh-side down, until well browned. Turn fish; cook until browned and just cooked through.

2   Meanwhile, place remaining oil, garlic, vinegar, chilli and parsley in small saucepan; stir over low heat until just warm – do not overheat. Spoon oil mixture over fish. Serve with lemon wedges and steamed zucchini and beans, if desired.

serves 4
per serving   18.2g fat; 1376kJ (329 cal)
tip   Sherry vinegar is available in some supermarkets; if unavailable, substitute red or white wine vinegar.

baked fish with ginger and soy

PREPARATION TIME **10 MINUTES**   COOKING TIME **25 MINUTES**

800g whole snapper
1 tablespoon finely grated fresh ginger
1 tablespoon peanut oil
¼ cup (60ml) chinese rice wine
¼ cup (60ml) light soy sauce
½ teaspoon sugar
3 green onions, sliced thinly

1 Cut three deep slits in each side of fish; place in oiled baking dish.
2 Rub ginger into fish; drizzle with combined oil, wine, soy sauce and sugar. Bake, covered, in moderately hot oven about 25 minutes or until fish is cooked. Serve fish drizzled with some of the pan juices and topped with onion.

serves 4
per serving 5.8g fat; 590kJ (141 cal)

prawn laksa

PREPARATION TIME **45 MINUTES**   COOKING TIME **1 HOUR 20 MINUTES**

2kg medium uncooked prawns
100g fresh coriander
4 trimmed sticks celery (300g), chopped coarsely
2 medium carrots (240g), chopped coarsely
2 large brown onions (400g), chopped coarsely
3 litres (12 cups) water
2 stalks lemon grass, chopped coarsely
3 fresh red thai chillies, seeded, chopped coarsely
1 teaspoon ground turmeric
¼ cup chopped fresh vietnamese mint
2 cloves garlic, crushed
1 tablespoon grated fresh ginger
1 tablespoon grated fresh galangal
1 tablespoon shrimp paste
1 tablespoon ground coriander
2 tablespoons peanut oil
400ml coconut milk
100g fresh singapore egg noodles
200g fried tofu
100g bean sprouts
4 green onions, sliced thinly

1 Shell and devein prawns; reserve prawns and shells. Cut roots from coriander. Wash leaves and roots well; reserve both but keep separate.
2 Combine reserved shells and coriander roots, celery, carrot and half of the brown onion with the water in large saucepan; bring to a boil. Reduce heat; simmer, uncovered, 30 minutes. Strain through muslin-lined strainer into large bowl. Reserve broth; discard shells and vegetables.
3 Blend or process remaining brown onion with ¼ cup loosely packed reserved coriander leaves, lemon grass, chilli, turmeric, mint, garlic, ginger, galangal, shrimp paste, ground coriander and half of the oil until mixture forms a paste.
4 Heat remaining oil in large saucepan; cook laksa paste, stirring, about 2 minutes or until fragrant. Stir in reserved broth and coconut milk; bring to a boil. Reduce heat; simmer, uncovered, 20 minutes. Stir in reserved prawns; cook, stirring, about 10 minutes or until prawns change in colour.
5 Meanwhile, place noodles in large heatproof bowl; cover with boiling water. Stand 3 minutes; drain. Cut tofu into 2cm cubes.
6 Just before serving, stir noodles, tofu, 2 tablespoons finely chopped reserved coriander leaves, sprouts and green onion into laksa.

serves 6
per serving 25.6g fat; 1926kJ (461 cal)
tip If you don't have access to packaged fried tofu, use fresh – cut tofu into cubes, then shallow-fry it in vegetable oil until browned lightly; drain on absorbent paper.

lime and chilli fish baked in banana leaves

PREPARATION TIME 25 MINUTES   COOKING TIME 15 MINUTES

2 large banana leaves
4 stalks lemon grass
4 fresh red thai chillies, seeded,
   sliced thinly
4 cloves garlic, crushed
1 tablespoon finely grated lime rind
$^1/_3$ cup (80ml) lime juice
2 tablespoons grated fresh ginger
1 cup chopped fresh coriander
1 cup (250ml) light coconut milk
8 x 150g ling fillets
cooking-oil spray
2 cups (400g) jasmine rice
4 green onions, sliced thinly

1 Preheat oven to hot.
2 Trim each banana leaf into four 30cm squares. Using metal tongs, dip one square at a time into large saucepan of boiling water; remove immediately. Rinse under cold running water; pat dry with absorbent paper. Banana leaf squares should be soft and pliable.
3 Halve lemon grass stalks. Combine chilli, garlic, rind, juice, ginger, coriander and coconut milk in small bowl.
4 Centre each fish fillet on banana leaf square. Top with lemon grass; drizzle with chilli mixture. Fold square over fish to enclose; secure each parcel with kitchen string.
5 Place parcels, in single layer, in large baking dish; coat with cooking-oil spray. Roast in hot oven about 10 minutes or until fish is cooked as desired.
6 Meanwhile, cook rice, uncovered, in large saucepan of boiling water until tender; drain. Stir onion through rice; serve with unwrapped fish parcels.

serves 8
per serving 7g fat; 1592kJ (381 cal)
tip Many supermarkets and greengrocers sell bundles of trimmed banana-leaf squares; they can also be used as placemats for an Asian meal. Use foil to wrap fish if banana leaves are unavailable.

hot and spicy fish cutlets

PREPARATION TIME **10 MINUTES (plus marinating time)** COOKING TIME **10 MINUTES**

4 white fish cutlets (1kg)

MARINADE
1 tablespoon paprika
2 teaspoons ground ginger
1 teaspoon curry powder
¼ teaspoon chilli powder
¼ cup (60ml) brown vinegar
¼ cup (60ml) tomato paste
1 cup (250ml) dry white wine
2 cloves garlic, crushed

1 Combine fish and marinade in large bowl. Cover; refrigerate 3 hours or overnight.
2 Remove fish from marinade; discard marinade.
3 Cook fish on heated oiled grill plate (or grill or barbecue) until cooked as desired; remove from pan. Serve with couscous and lemon, if desired.

marinade Combine ingredients in medium bowl; mix well.

serves 4
per serving 5g fat; 1134kJ (271 cal)
tip Fish is best marinated a day ahead and refrigerated, covered; uncooked marinated fish is suitable to freeze.

garlic prawns and bok choy with herbed rice

PREPARATION TIME **20 MINUTES**   COOKING TIME **15 MINUTES**

36 medium uncooked prawns (1kg)
6 cloves garlic, crushed
2 teaspoons finely chopped fresh coriander
3 fresh red thai chillies, seeded, chopped finely
$^1/_3$ cup (80ml) lime juice
1 teaspoon sugar
1 tablespoon peanut oil
1kg baby bok choy, quartered lengthways
6 green onions, sliced thinly
1 tablespoon sweet chilli sauce

HERBED RICE
2 cups (400g) jasmine rice
2 tablespoons chopped fresh coriander
1 tablespoon chopped fresh mint
1 tablespoon chopped fresh flat-leaf parsley
1 teaspoon finely grated lime rind

1 Shell and devein prawns, leaving tails intact.
2 Combine prawns in large bowl with garlic, coriander, chilli, juice and sugar.
3 Heat half of the oil in wok or large non-stick frying pan; stir-fry prawns, in batches, until just changed in colour.
4 Heat remaining oil with pan liquids in wok; stir-fry bok choy, onion and sauce, in batches, until just tender. Combine bok choy mixture and prawns in wok; stir-fry until hot. Serve prawns on herbed rice.

herbed rice Cook rice, uncovered, in large saucepan of boiling water until tender; drain. Return rice to pan; combine with remaining ingredients.

serves 6
per serving 4.5g fat; 1602kJ (383 cal)

manhattan clam chowder

PREPARATION TIME **25 MINUTES**   COOKING TIME **35 MINUTES**

1.5kg clams

1 cup (250ml) dry white wine

40g butter

1 medium brown onion (150g),
   chopped finely

2 bacon rashers (140g), chopped finely

2 trimmed sticks celery (150g),
   chopped finely

¹/₄ cup (35g) plain flour

3 cups (750ml) fish stock

400g can tomatoes

3 cups (750ml) water

1 tablespoon fresh thyme leaves

2 bay leaves

4 large potatoes (1.2kg), cut into
   1cm cubes

¹/₄ cup chopped fresh flat-leaf parsley

1   Rinse clams under cold running water. Combine with wine in medium saucepan having a tight-fitting lid; bring to a boil. Steam, covered tightly, about 5 minutes or until clams have opened; discard any that do not open. Strain clams over large bowl; reserve ¼ cup (60ml) of the cooking liquid.

2   Melt butter in large saucepan; cook onion, stirring, until soft. Add bacon and celery; cook, stirring, 5 minutes. Add flour; cook, stirring, until mixture thickens and bubbles. Gradually stir in stock. Add undrained crushed tomatoes and the water; cook, stirring, until mixture boils and thickens. Stir in thyme, bay leaves and potato; cook, covered, stirring occasionally, about 15 minutes or until potato is tender.

3   Just before serving, stir clams, reserved cooking liquid and parsley into chowder.

serves 6

per serving 8g fat; 1190kJ (285 cal)

tips Dry red wine can be substituted for the white wine but be certain that whatever wine you use you would also consider drinking.
Cubed raw potato won't discolour if submerged in cold water until required.

smoked salmon and caviar salad

PREPARATION TIME **15 MINUTES**   COOKING TIME **30 MINUTES**

1.2kg kipfler potatoes
1 tablespoon olive oil
500g fresh asparagus, trimmed
400g finely sliced smoked salmon
100g mesclun
25g red caviar

AVOCADO PUREE
1 small avocado (200g)
¹/₄ cup (60g) sour cream
1 tablespoon chopped fresh dill
2 tablespoons lime juice

1 Boil, steam or microwave potatoes until just tender; drain. Preheat oven to very hot.
2 Halve potatoes; place, cut-side up, on lightly oiled oven tray. Drizzle with oil; bake, uncovered, in very hot oven about 15 minutes or until crisp and brown, turning occasionally.
3 Boil, steam or microwave asparagus until just tender; drain, cut spears in half crossways.
4 Cut salmon slices into strips.
5 Divide avocado puree among serving plates; top with potato, mesclun, asparagus, salmon and caviar.

avocado puree Halve avocado; discard stone. Scoop out flesh and chop coarsely; blend or process avocado with remaining ingredients until smooth.

serves 4
per serving 24.2g fat; 2216kJ (530 cal)
tip Kipflers are small, bumpy, finger-shaped potatoes with a nutty flavour; they are particularly well-suited for salads that contain oven-roasted potatoes.

steamed coconut fish

PREPARATION TIME **10 MINUTES**   COOKING TIME **25 MINUTES**

2 cups chopped fresh coriander
2 fresh red thai chillies, chopped coarsely
2 cloves garlic, quartered
20g fresh ginger, peeled, chopped coarsely
1 tablespoon cumin seeds
$^2/_3$ cup (50g) shredded coconut
1 tablespoon peanut oil
4 medium whole snapper (1.8kg)

1 Blend or process coriander, chilli, garlic, ginger and seeds until chopped finely.
2 Combine coriander mixture with coconut and oil in small bowl; mix well.
3 Score each fish three times both sides; place fish on large sheet of foil. Press coconut mixture onto fish; fold foil over to enclose fish.
4 Place fish in large bamboo steamer; steam fish, covered, over wok or large saucepan of simmering water about 25 minutes or until cooked through. Serve with lemon wedges, steamed long-grain white rice and stir-fried bok choy, if desired.

serves 4
per serving 15.8g fat; 1237kJ (296 cal)
tips Prick the foil with a skewer to allow steam to escape.
Score fish by making shallow cuts in a criss-cross pattern, to allow the herbs and spices to penetrate the flesh and enhance flavour.
We used snapper in this recipe, but you can use any whole white-fleshed fish, such as bream or flathead.
You will need a piece of ginger about 3cm long for this recipe.

chicken

One of the most versatile of ingredients, chicken is perfectly suited to casual eating. Noodle wedges with smoked chicken, green chicken curry, or honey chilli chicken – whatever flavours you prefer, the result will be delicious every time.

honey chilli chicken

PREPARATION TIME **15 MINUTES**   COOKING TIME **25 MINUTES**

vegetable oil, for deep-frying
100g bean thread vermicelli
1 teaspoon chilli oil
3 teaspoons peanut oil
2 medium brown onions (300g), sliced thinly
4 cloves garlic, crushed
1 tablespoon grated fresh ginger
1kg chicken thigh fillets, halved
½ cup (180g) honey
2 tablespoons sweet chilli sauce
500g chinese broccoli, chopped coarsely
¼ cup coarsely chopped fresh garlic chives

1   Heat vegetable oil in wok or large frying pan. Deep-fry noodles, in batches, until puffed and white; drain on absorbent paper.
2   Heat chilli oil and peanut oil in wok or large frying pan; stir-fry onion, garlic and ginger until fragrant. Add chicken, honey and sauce; stir-fry until chicken is browned and cooked through. Add broccoli and chives; stir-fry until broccoli is just tender. Serve over noodles.

serves 4
per serving   27.7g fat; 2681kJ (641 cal)

pesto chicken with salsa

PREPARATION TIME 15 MINUTES (plus marinating and cooling times) COOKING TIME 25 MINUTES

1kg chicken tenderloins
³/₄ cup (195g) sun-dried tomato pesto

SALSA
4 medium tomatoes (760g)
6 green onions, sliced thinly
1 medium red onion (170g),
   chopped finely
2 tablespoons lemon juice
1 tablespoon olive oil
¹/₂ teaspoon freshly ground black pepper

1 Trim chicken. Combine chicken and pesto in large bowl. Cover; marinate in refrigerator 3 hours or overnight.

2 Preheat oven to hot. Place chicken on wire rack over baking dish; cook, uncovered, in hot oven about 25 minutes or until chicken is cooked and tender. Cool 5 minutes; refrigerate until cold. Slice chicken and serve with salsa.

salsa Remove seeds from tomatoes; chop tomatoes finely. Combine tomato with remaining ingredients in medium bowl.

serves 4
per serving 26g fat; 2142kJ (512 cal)
tip We used vine-ripened tomatoes in our salsa, however any variety of tomato can be used.

thai basil chicken stir-fry

PREPARATION TIME 20 MINUTES (plus marinating time)   COOKING TIME 20 MINUTES

1 teaspoon sesame oil
$^1/_2$ cup (125ml) light soy sauce
$^1/_4$ cup (90g) honey
$^1/_4$ cup (60ml) lime juice
3 fresh red thai chillies, seeded, sliced thinly
2 teaspoons cornflour
850g chicken breast fillets, sliced thinly
2 tablespoons peanut oil
3 cloves garlic, crushed
2 large red onions (600g), sliced thinly
240g fresh baby corn
2 teaspoons finely grated lime rind
3 cups (240g) bean sprouts
2 cups loosely packed fresh thai basil leaves
1 cup loosely packed fresh coriander leaves

1 Combine sesame oil, sauce, honey, juice, chilli and cornflour in large bowl. Add chicken; toss to coat in marinade. Cover; refrigerate 3 hours or overnight.
2 Drain chicken over medium bowl; reserve marinade.
3 Heat half of the peanut oil in wok or large non-stick frying pan; stir-fry chicken, in batches, until browned all over. Heat remaining peanut oil in wok; stir-fry garlic, onion and corn until just tender. Return chicken to wok with reserved marinade and rind; stir-fry until sauce boils and chicken is cooked through.
4 Remove from heat; add sprouts, basil and coriander. Toss with chicken and vegetables until combined. Serve with steamed jasmine rice and wedges of fresh lime, if desired.

serves 8
per serving 11.5g fat; 1219kJ (292 cal)
tip Grate rind from lime before juicing it.

green chicken curry

PREPARATION TIME 25 MINUTES   COOKING TIME 15 MINUTES

750g chicken thigh fillets, sliced thinly
200g green beans, chopped coarsely
1 cup (250ml) coconut cream

GREEN CURRY PASTE
3 fresh green thai chillies,
   chopped finely
3 green onions, chopped finely
2 cloves garlic, crushed
$^1/_4$ cup finely chopped fresh
   lemon grass
$^1/_4$ cup chopped fresh coriander
2 tablespoons peanut oil
2 tablespoons water
1 teaspoon shrimp paste
$^1/_2$ teaspoon ground cumin
$^1/_4$ teaspoon ground turmeric

1 Cook green curry paste in large heated saucepan, stirring, about 3 minutes or until fragrant.

2 Add chicken and beans to pan; cook, stirring, about 5 minutes or until chicken is tender. Stir in coconut cream; simmer, uncovered, about 3 minutes or until slightly thickened. Top with sliced green onion, if desired.

green curry paste Blend or process ingredients until smooth.

serves 4
per serving 30.4g fat; 1898kJ (454 cal)
tip Curry is best made just before serving. Paste can be made a week ahead and refrigerated, covered.

noodle wedges with smoked chicken

PREPARATION TIME 35 MINUTES (plus standing and refrigeration times)   COOKING TIME 15 MINUTES

250g thin fresh egg noodles
1 tablespoon polenta
2 tablespoons olive oil
150g snow peas
150g green beans
4 green onions
400g coarsely shredded
   smoked chicken

LIME AND CHILLI DRESSING
$^1/_2$ cup (125ml) peanut oil
$^1/_3$ cup (80ml) lime juice
1 tablespoon sweet chilli sauce
1 tablespoon hoisin sauce

1 Place noodles in large heatproof bowl; cover with boiling water. Stand 3 minutes; drain.
2 Sprinkle polenta over base of oiled deep 19cm-square cake pan. Press cooled noodles firmly into pan. Cover; refrigerate 3 hours or overnight.
3 Turn noodle cake onto board; cut into quarters. Heat oil in large frying pan; cook noodle squares, in batches, until browned lightly both sides. Drain on absorbent paper; cut each square into two triangles.
4 Slice snow peas diagonally; cut beans into 5cm lengths. Boil, steam or microwave snow peas and beans, separately, until just tender; drain. Cut onions into long thin strips.
5 Toss peas, beans and onion in large bowl with chicken. Divide noodle wedges among plates. Top with chicken salad; drizzle with dressing.

lime and chilli dressing Combine ingredients in screw-top jar; shake well.

serves 4
per serving 48.8g fat; 3347kJ (801 cal)
tips Dressing can be made a day ahead and refrigerated, covered.
A purchased barbecue chicken can be substituted for the smoked chicken.

stir-fried noodles, chicken and bok choy

PREPARATION TIME **10 MINUTES**   COOKING TIME **20 MINUTES**

250g dried thin rice noodles
1 tablespoon peanut oil
3 eggs, beaten lightly
1 medium brown onion (150g), chopped finely
2 cloves garlic, crushed
2 tablespoons grated fresh ginger
500g chicken mince
500g baby bok choy, chopped coarsely
¼ cup (60ml) light soy sauce
½ cup chopped fresh coriander
3 cups (240g) bean sprouts

1   Place noodles in large heatproof bowl; cover with boiling water. Stand until just tender; drain.
2   Brush heated wok or large frying pan with a little of the oil. Add half of the egg; swirl to cover base of wok. Cook, covered, about 3 minutes or until cooked through. Remove omelette from wok; repeat with remaining egg. Roll omelettes tightly; slice thinly.
3   Heat remaining oil in wok; stir-fry onion, garlic and ginger until onion softens. Add chicken; stir-fry until chicken is cooked through.
4   Add bok choy, sauce and coriander; stir-fry until bok choy is just tender. Stir in noodles and sprouts; serve immediately, topped with omelette.

serves 4
per serving   19.8g fat; 2149kJ (514 cal)
tips   Create a vegetarian version of this dish by substituting fried tofu for the chicken.
You can substitute choy sum, chinese broccoli or trimmed, thinly sliced bok choy for the baby bok choy.

chicken and snake beans with thai basil

PREPARATION TIME 5 MINUTES   COOKING TIME 15 MINUTES

700g snake beans
1 tablespoon peanut oil
880g chicken thigh fillets,
    chopped coarsely
2 medium white onions (300g),
    sliced thickly
3 cloves garlic, crushed
1 teaspoon five-spice powder
¹/₂ cup (125ml) oyster sauce
2 tablespoons light soy sauce
¹/₂ cup (75g) cashews, toasted
¹/₂ cup loosely packed thai basil leaves

1 Cut snake beans into 5cm lengths.
2 Heat half of the oil in wok or large frying pan; stir-fry chicken, in batches, until browned all over and cooked through.
3 Heat remaining oil in wok; stir-fry onion, garlic and five-spice until onion softens. Add beans; stir-fry until beans are tender. Return chicken to wok with sauces and nuts; stir-fry until sauce boils and thickens slightly. Just before serving, stir in basil. Serve with noodles, if desired.

serves 4
per serving 30.7g fat; 2353kJ (563 cal)
tip Green beans can be substituted for the snake beans, and sweet basil can be substituted for the thai basil, if unavailable.

cajun chicken with tomato salsa

PREPARATION TIME 20 MINUTES   COOKING TIME 15 MINUTES

750g chicken breast fillets, sliced thinly
$^1/_4$ cup (18g) cajun seasoning
2 teaspoons grated lime rind
2 trimmed corn cobs (500g)
2 tablespoons olive oil
1 small red onion (100g), cut into
**   thin wedges**

TOMATO SALSA
2 small egg tomatoes (120g),
**   chopped finely**
2 green onions, sliced thinly
2 teaspoons lime juice
2 teaspoons balsamic vinegar

1   Combine chicken, seasoning and rind in large bowl; mix well. Cut kernels from corn.
2   Heat half of the oil in wok or large frying pan; stir-fry chicken mixture, in batches, until cooked through.
3   Heat remaining oil in wok; stir-fry corn and onion until onion is soft.
4   Return chicken to wok; stir-fry until hot.
5   Serve chicken mixture topped with tomato salsa.

tomato salsa   Combine ingredients in small bowl; mix well.

serves 4
per serving   21.2g fat; 1877kJ (449 cal)
tip   Recipe best made just before serving; serve with sour cream, if desired.

moroccan chicken with beetroot puree and couscous

PREPARATION TIME 30 MINUTES (plus marinating time)   COOKING TIME 1 HOUR

8 single chicken breast fillets (1.4kg)
1 tablespoon olive oil
2 teaspoons finely grated lemon rind
2 tablespoons lemon juice
2 cloves garlic, crushed
1 tablespoon ground coriander
1 tablespoon ground cumin
2 teaspoons ground cardamom
1 teaspoon sweet paprika
1 teaspoon ground turmeric
1/2 cup chopped fresh flat-leaf parsley
1/4 cup chopped fresh coriander
2 cups (400g) couscous
2 cups (500ml) boiling water
1/4 cup chopped fresh mint

BEETROOT PUREE
6 medium beetroot (1kg), trimmed
1/2 cup (140g) low-fat yogurt

1 Combine chicken, oil, rind, juice, garlic, spices, parsley and fresh coriander in large bowl. Cover; marinate in refrigerator 1 hour.
2 Prepare beetroot puree.
3 Combine couscous and the water in large heatproof bowl. Cover; stand about 5 minutes or until the water is absorbed, fluffing couscous with fork occasionally to separate grains. Add mint; toss gently with fork to combine.
4 Cook undrained chicken, in batches, in large heated lightly oiled non-stick frying pan until browned both sides and cooked through. Slice chicken and serve on couscous; top with beetroot puree.

beetroot puree Preheat oven to moderate. Wrap unpeeled beetroot in foil. Place on oven tray; roast in moderate oven about 1 hour or until tender. When cool enough to handle, peel beetroot; chop coarsely. Blend or process beetroot until pureed. Stir in yogurt; cover to keep warm.

serves 8
per serving 13g fat; 2133kJ (510 cal)
tip Cardamom pods should be bruised with the side of a heavy knife until crushed just to the point of opening; the seeds can then be extracted and used, whole or ground.

vegetarian

There are so many choices when it comes to mouth-watering vegetarian food – from rich, flavoursome dishes to light, healthy meals. Try the red onion, cheese and vegetable frittata, gnocchi with roasted pumpkin and burnt butter, or the free-form spinach and ricotta pie.

gnocchi with roasted pumpkin and burnt butter

PREPARATION TIME **5 MINUTES**   COOKING TIME **15 MINUTES**

From the Italian word for dumplings, gnocchi are little balls of dough – great for soaking up pasta sauces. You will need to buy a piece of pumpkin weighing about 650g to make this recipe.

500g trimmed pumpkin
1kg gnocchi
100g butter
1 tablespoon olive oil
1 clove garlic, crushed
1 tablespoon shredded fresh sage

1 Preheat oven to moderate.
2 Cut pumpkin into 1cm cubes. Place on oiled oven tray; roast, uncovered, in moderate oven about 15 minutes or until just tender.
3 Meanwhile, cook gnocchi in large saucepan of boiling water, uncovered, until just tender; drain. Keep warm.
4 Melt butter with oil in medium frying pan; cook garlic, stirring, 2 minutes. Add sage; cook, stirring, until butter foams.
5 Combine pumpkin, gnocchi and butter mixture in large bowl; stir gently.

serves 4
per serving 27.8g fat; 2634kJ (630 cal)
tip Pumpkin can be cooked in the microwave oven to reduce cooking time.

chickpea corn enchiladas

PREPARATION TIME **15 MINUTES**   COOKING TIME **10 MINUTES**

1 tablespoon olive oil

1 small brown onion (80g),
   chopped coarsely

1 clove garlic, crushed

1 teaspoon sweet paprika

¹/₂ teaspoon ground chilli powder

1 teaspoon ground cumin

400g can tomato puree

300g can chickpeas, rinsed, drained

1 tablespoon chopped fresh coriander

8 corn tortillas

1 small red onion (100g), chopped coarsely

1 medium tomato (190g), chopped coarsely

1 small avocado (200g), chopped coarsely

¹/₂ cup (60g) coarsely grated
   cheddar cheese

¹/₂ cup finely shredded iceberg lettuce

1 Heat oil in medium saucepan; cook onion and garlic, stirring, until onion softens. Add spices; cook, stirring, 2 minutes. Add puree; bring to a boil. Reduce heat; simmer, stirring occasionally, 5 minutes. Add chickpeas and coriander; cook, stirring, until hot.

2 Soften tortillas in microwave oven on HIGH (100%) for 30 seconds. Divide chickpea mixture and remaining ingredients among tortillas; fold enchiladas to enclose filling.

serves 4

per serving 21.2g fat; 1972kJ (472 cal)

tips We used 16cm-round corn tortillas, which are packaged in cryovac. Unused tortillas can be frozen in freezer bags for up to 3 weeks. You can also soften tortillas by wrapping them in foil and heating them in a moderate oven about 5 minutes or until hot.

garlic roast capsicums with olive croutes

PREPARATION TIME **15 MINUTES**   COOKING TIME **1 HOUR 40 MINUTES**

1 medium red onion (170g)
2 medium red capsicums (400g)
2 medium green capsicums (400g)
2 medium yellow capsicums (400g)
$\frac{1}{2}$ cup (125ml) olive oil
10 unpeeled cloves garlic
$\frac{1}{3}$ cup (50g) pine nuts, toasted
150g fetta cheese

TOMATO SALSA
1 medium red onion (170g)
400g can tomatoes
$\frac{1}{2}$ teaspoon sugar
$\frac{1}{3}$ cup (80ml) water

OLIVE CROUTES
1 large loaf crusty bread
$\frac{1}{2}$ cup (125ml) olive oil
$\frac{1}{4}$ cup (65g) olive paste

1 Preheat oven to moderate.
2 Cut onion into eight wedges. Quarter capsicums; remove and discard seeds and membranes.
3 Combine onion, capsicum, oil and garlic in large baking dish; bake, uncovered, in moderate oven 1 hour.
4 Add tomato salsa and pine nuts; bake 30 minutes, turning vegetables occasionally.
5 Serve vegetables with crumbled cheese and olive croutes.

tomato salsa Cut onion into eight wedges. Combine onion, undrained crushed tomatoes and remaining ingredients in large saucepan; simmer, uncovered, until thickened.
olive croutes Cut bread into 1.5cm slices; place bread on oven tray. Brush with combined oil and paste; toast in moderately hot oven about 10 minutes.

serves 4
per serving 75.2g fat; 4082kJ (976 cal)
tip Recipe can be prepared a day ahead. Vegetables should be refrigerated, covered, and croutes stored in an airtight container.

spinach and cheese quesadillas

PREPARATION TIME **20 MINUTES** COOKING TIME **10 MINUTES**

Quesadillas are filled tortillas which are grilled or fried and served with fresh salsa. We used small flour tortillas measuring approximately 16cm in diameter; they are sometimes labelled "fajita tortillas" on the package.

²/₃ cup (130g) low-fat cottage cheese
100g spinach leaves, trimmed
1 medium avocado (250g), chopped finely
1 cup (200g) canned mexican-style beans, drained
125g can corn kernels, drained
2 medium tomatoes (380g), seeded, chopped finely
1 small red onion (100g), chopped finely
2 medium zucchini (240g), grated coarsely
16 small flour tortillas
1¹/₂ cups (150g) coarsely grated low-fat mozzarella cheese

1 Blend or process cottage cheese and spinach until smooth. Combine avocado, beans, corn, tomato, onion and zucchini in medium bowl.
2 Place eight tortillas on lightly oiled oven tray; divide spinach mixture among tortillas, leaving 2cm border around edge. Divide avocado mixture among tortillas, sprinkling it over spinach mixture. Top each with one of the remaining tortillas.
3 Sprinkle mozzarella over quesadilla stacks; place under preheated grill until cheese just melts and browns lightly.

serves 8
per serving 11.8g fat; 1177kJ (282 cal)

red onion, cheese and vegetable frittata

PREPARATION TIME 15 MINUTES   COOKING TIME 25 MINUTES

2 tablespoons olive oil
2 medium red onions (340g), sliced thinly
1 clove garlic, crushed
2 medium green zucchini (240g), grated
250g button mushrooms, sliced thinly
1 tablespoon chopped fresh chives
2 tablespoons chopped fresh basil
1 teaspoon freshly ground black pepper
8 eggs, beaten lightly
1 cup (100g) grated mozzarella cheese

1 Heat oil in 23cm non-stick frying pan; cook onion and garlic, stirring, until onion is soft.
2 Stir in zucchini and mushroom. Cook, stirring, until vegetables are tender; stir in herbs and pepper. Reduce heat; pour in egg.
3 Cook egg mixture over low heat, without stirring, until base is browned lightly and top is almost set; sprinkle with cheese. Place pan under grill on high heat until top is set and browned lightly. Cut into wedges.
4 Serve with salad, if desired.

serves 4
per serving 25.6g fat; 1488kJ (356 cal)
tip This recipe is best made just before serving.

free-form spinach and ricotta pie

PREPARATION TIME **10 MINUTES**   COOKING TIME **30 MINUTES**

Taking the Greek pie, spanakopita, as our inspiration, we've simplified the recipe by replacing the traditional fillo pastry with ready-rolled puff pastry.

200g baby spinach leaves
2 tablespoons olive oil
1 medium brown onion (150g), chopped coarsely
1 clove garlic, crushed
2 teaspoons finely grated lemon rind
$^1/_4$ cup chopped fresh flat-leaf parsley
$^1/_4$ cup chopped fresh dill
2 tablespoons chopped fresh mint
1$^1/_2$ cups (300g) ricotta cheese
2 sheets ready-rolled puff pastry

1 Preheat oven to very hot.
2 Boil, steam or microwave spinach until just wilted; drain on absorbent paper. Squeeze out excess liquid.
3 Heat oil in small frying pan; cook onion and garlic until onion softens.
4 Combine spinach, onion mixture, rind, herbs and cheese in large bowl; mix well.
5 Oil two oven trays and place in oven about 5 minutes to heat. Place a sheet of pastry on each tray; divide spinach mixture between sheets, leaving a 3cm border. Using a metal spatula, fold pastry border roughly over edge of filling.
6 Bake pies in very hot oven about 20 minutes or until pastry browns.

serves 4
per serving 36.8g fat; 2184kJ (522 cal)
tip For best results, use a pizza tray with holes in the base – this will make it possible to cook the pastry evenly.

grilled haloumi, tomato and eggplant salad

PREPARATION TIME **20 MINUTES** COOKING TIME **25 MINUTES**

¹/₂ **cup (125ml) olive oil**
4 baby eggplants (240g), sliced thinly
4 medium egg tomatoes (300g),
    halved lengthways
400g haloumi cheese, sliced thinly
250g rocket, chopped coarsely
¹/₄ **cup firmly packed fresh**
    basil leaves
2 tablespoons red wine vinegar
2 teaspoons chopped drained capers

1 Heat 1 tablespoon of the oil in large frying pan or grill pan. Cook eggplant until browned both sides; remove from pan.

2 Add tomato to same pan; cook, cut-side down, until browned and softened slightly. Remove from pan.

3 Heat another tablespoon of the oil in same pan; cook haloumi until browned lightly both sides.

4 Combine eggplant, tomato, haloumi, rocket and basil in large bowl with remaining oil, vinegar and capers.

serves 4
per serving 59.1g fat; 2681kJ (641 cal)
tip This recipe is best made just before serving.

roasted vegetable fillo tart

PREPARATION TIME 20 MINUTES   COOKING TIME 55 MINUTES

6 medium egg tomatoes
   (450g), quartered
1 small red onion (100g),
   sliced thickly
2 small yellow capsicums (300g)
2 small red capsicums (300g)
100g low-fat fetta cheese, crumbled
1 tablespoon shredded fresh basil
9 sheets fillo pastry
cooking-oil spray

1   Preheat oven to moderately hot.
2   Combine tomato and onion in baking dish; roast in moderately hot oven, uncovered, about 40 minutes or until onion softens.
3   Meanwhile, quarter capsicums; remove and discard seeds and membranes. Roast under grill or in moderately hot oven, skin-side up, until skin blisters and blackens; cover capsicum with plastic or paper 5 minutes. Peel away and discard skin; slice capsicum flesh thinly. Place capsicum, cheese and basil in baking dish with tomato mixture; stir gently to combine.
4   Stack sheets of fillo; spray with cooking-oil spray every third sheet. Carefully fold over all four edges of the stack to create 18cm x 30cm tart "shell".
5   Fill tart shell with vegetable mixture, spreading it to an even thickness; bake, uncovered, in moderately hot oven about 15 minutes or until pastry is browned lightly.

serves 6
per serving 4.4g fat; 450kJ (108 cal)
tip Keep fillo covered with a damp tea towel to prevent the sheets from drying out before use.

slow food

From the tender, braised veal of osso buco to the succulent slow-roasted salmon with asian greens, these melt-in-the-mouth recipes prove that time taken in the preparation of a dish can have its ultimate rewards.

roast leg of lamb with gravy

PREPARATION TIME **10 MINUTES** (plus standing time)   COOKING TIME **2 HOURS**

20g fresh rosemary
2kg leg of lamb
2 cloves garlic, each cut into 8 slices
$^{1}/_{4}$ cup (60ml) olive oil
40g butter
1 small brown onion (80g), chopped finely
2 tablespoons plain flour
$^{1}/_{2}$ cup (125ml) dry red wine
1$^{1}/_{2}$ cups (375ml) lamb stock

1 Preheat oven to hot.
2 Reserve 16 similar-size rosemary sprigs; place remaining rosemary in large flameproof baking dish.
3 Remove and discard as much excess fat from lamb as possible. Pierce surface of lamb all over, making 16 small cuts with a sharp knife; press a garlic slice and a rosemary sprig into each cut.
4 Place lamb on top of rosemary in baking dish. Pour oil over lamb; roast, uncovered, in hot oven 20 minutes. Reduce temperature to moderate; roast lamb further 1½ hours, spooning over pan juices occasionally. Remove lamb from dish; stand 5 minutes before slicing.
5 Drain juices from dish. Melt butter in dish over low heat; cook onion, stirring, until soft. Stir in flour; cook, stirring, about 5 minutes or until browned. Pour in wine and stock; cook over high heat, stirring, until gravy boils and thickens. Strain gravy; serve with lamb.

serves 6
per serving 26.3g fat; 2038kJ (488 cal)
tip Beef stock can be substituted for lamb stock, if unavailable.

slow-roasted salmon with asian greens

PREPARATION TIME **15 MINUTES**   COOKING TIME **40 MINUTES**

750g piece salmon fillet, boned,
   with skin on
1 fresh kaffir lime, quartered
1 tablespoon finely shredded kaffir
   lime leaves
1 tablespoon peanut oil
250g fresh asparagus, trimmed,
   chopped coarsely
150g snow peas
150g baby bok choy, chopped coarsely
150g choy sum, chopped coarsely

CHILLI SAUCE
$^1/_2$ cup (110g) caster sugar
$^1/_4$ cup (60ml) lime juice
$^1/_4$ cup (60ml) water
2 fresh red thai chillies, seeded,
   chopped finely
$^1/_4$ cup firmly packed fresh coriander

1 Preheat oven to very slow.
2 Cook fish and lime on heated oiled grill plate (or grill or barbecue) until both are lightly coloured all over. Place fish and lime in large oiled baking dish; sprinkle with lime leaves. Bake, covered tightly, in very slow oven about 30 minutes or until cooked as desired.
3 Heat oil in wok or large frying pan; stir-fry asparagus and snow peas until just tender. Add bok choy and choy sum with half of the chilli sauce; stir-fry until leaves are just wilted.
4 Serve vegetables with fish, drizzled with remaining chilli sauce.

chilli sauce Combine sugar, juice and the water in small saucepan; stir over heat, without boiling, until sugar dissolves. Simmer, uncovered, without stirring, 3 minutes; cool slightly. Stir in chilli and coriander.

serves 4
per serving 16.3g fat; 1686kJ (403 cal)

lamb and apricot tagine with citrus couscous

PREPARATION TIME 20 MINUTES (plus standing time)
COOKING TIME 1 HOUR

1^2/$_3$ cups (250g) dried apricots
^{3}/$_4$ cup (180ml) orange juice
^{1}/$_2$ cup (125ml) boiling water
2 tablespoons olive oil
900g lamb steaks, chopped coarsely
2 medium red capsicums (400g), chopped coarsely
1 large brown onion (200g), chopped coarsely
2 medium kumara (800g), chopped coarsely
3 cloves garlic, crushed
1 teaspoon ground cinnamon
2 teaspoons ground cumin
2 teaspoons ground coriander
1 cup (250ml) dry red wine
1 litre (4 cups) chicken stock
2 tablespoons honey
1 cup loosely packed fresh coriander leaves
^{3}/$_4$ cup (200g) low-fat yogurt

CITRUS COUSCOUS
1 litre (4 cups) water
4 cups (800g) couscous
1 tablespoon finely grated orange rind
2 teaspoons finely grated lemon rind
2 teaspoons finely grated lime rind

1 Combine apricots, juice and the water in small bowl. Cover; allow to stand 45 minutes.

2 Meanwhile, heat half of the oil in large saucepan; cook lamb, in batches, until browned all over.

3 Heat remaining oil in same pan; cook capsicum, onion, kumara, garlic and ground spices, stirring, until onion softens and mixture is fragrant. Add wine; bring to a boil. Reduce heat; simmer, uncovered, about 5 minutes or until liquid reduces by half.

4 Return lamb to pan with undrained apricots, stock and honey; bring to a boil. Reduce heat; simmer, covered, about 50 minutes or until lamb is tender. Remove from heat; stir in fresh coriander.

5 Serve lamb and apricot tagine on citrus couscous; drizzle with yogurt.

citrus couscous Bring the water to a boil in medium saucepan; stir in couscous and rinds. Remove from heat; stand, covered, about 5 minutes or until liquid is absorbed, fluffing with fork occasionally to separate grains.

serves 8
per serving 12.8g fat; 1837kJ (439 cal)

lamb with madeira and olive sauce

PREPARATION TIME **15 MINUTES**   COOKING TIME **1 HOUR 45 MINUTES**

1 teaspoon vegetable oil
8 frenched lamb shanks (1.2kg)
4 medium brown onions (600g),
**   chopped finely**
8 cloves garlic, peeled
¼ cup (30g) seeded black
**   olives, quartered**
2 tablespoons tomato paste
6 medium egg tomatoes (450g), halved
1 cup (250ml) beef stock
½ cup (125ml) madeira
2 teaspoons dried rosemary leaves

1 Preheat oven to moderate.
2 Heat oil in 3-litre (12-cup) flameproof casserole dish. Cook lamb, in batches, until browned all over. Cook onion and garlic in dish, stirring, until onion is soft.
3 Return lamb to dish. Add olive, paste, tomato, stock, madeira and rosemary; cook, uncovered, in moderate oven 1½ hours or until lamb is tender.

serves 8
per serving 25g fat; 1832kJ (438 cal)
tip Recipe can be made a day ahead and refrigerated, covered; suitable to freeze.

chicken cacciatore

PREPARATION TIME 30 MINUTES (plus standing time)   COOKING TIME 1 HOUR 20 MINUTES

2 tablespoons olive oil

1.5kg chicken pieces

1 medium brown onion (150g),
    chopped finely

1 clove garlic, crushed

$^1/_2$ cup (125ml) dry white wine

1$^1/_2$ tablespoons vinegar

$^1/_2$ cup (125ml) chicken stock

400g can tomatoes

1 tablespoon tomato paste

1 teaspoon finely chopped fresh basil

1 teaspoon sugar

3 anchovy fillets, chopped finely

$^1/_4$ cup (60ml) milk

$^1/_2$ cup (60g) seeded black olives, halved

2 tablespoons chopped fresh
    flat-leaf parsley

1 Preheat oven to moderate.

2 Heat oil in large frying pan; cook chicken until browned all over. Place chicken in ovenproof dish.

3 Pour off most pan juices, leaving about 1 tablespoon in pan. Add onion and garlic to pan; cook until onion is soft. Add wine and vinegar; bring to a boil. Boil until reduced by half. Add stock; stir over high heat 2 minutes. Push tomatoes with their liquid through sieve; add to pan with paste, basil and sugar. Cook further 1 minute.

4 Pour tomato mixture over chicken pieces. Cover; cook in moderate oven 1 hour.

5 Soak anchovy in milk 5 minutes; drain on absorbent paper. Arrange chicken pieces in serving dish; keep warm. Pour pan juices into medium saucepan. Bring to a boil; boil 1 minute. Add anchovy, olive and half of the parsley to pan; cook 1 minute. Pour sauce over chicken pieces. Sprinkle with remaining parsley.

serves 4

per serving 42.2g fat; 2571kJ (615 cal)

madras lamb with roti

PREPARATION TIME **50 MINUTES**   COOKING TIME **2 HOURS**

2 tablespoons peanut oil
1.5kg diced lamb
2 medium brown onions (300g), chopped coarsely
2 cloves garlic, crushed
1 tablespoon ground cumin
2 tablespoons ground coriander
2 teaspoons garam masala
1 teaspoon chilli powder
1 cinnamon stick
5 medium tomatoes (1kg), chopped coarsely
3 cups (750ml) beef stock
400ml coconut cream

ROTI
1½ cups (225g) besan
1½ cups (240g) wholemeal plain flour
1½ cups (225g) plain flour
1½ teaspoons salt
80g ghee
2 tablespoons chopped fresh coriander
1 cup (250ml) warm water, approximately

1 Heat half of the oil in large heavy-base saucepan; cook lamb, in batches, until browned all over.

2 Heat remaining oil in same pan; cook onion and garlic, stirring, until onion is soft. Add spices, chilli and cinnamon; cook, stirring, about 2 minutes or until fragrant.

3 Return lamb to pan with tomato and stock; bring to a boil. Reduce heat; simmer, uncovered, 1½ hours.

4 Add coconut cream; simmer, uncovered, about 10 minutes or until sauce is just thickened. Discard cinnamon stick. Serve curry with roti.

roti Sift flours and salt into large bowl; rub in ghee. Stir in coriander and just enough of the water to form a soft dough. Knead on floured surface about 5 minutes or until dough is smooth and elastic. Divide dough into 16 pieces; roll each piece into a 17cm-round roti. During preparation, stack rotis between pieces of plastic wrap; cover completely with plastic wrap to avoid rotis drying out. Cook rotis, in batches, on heated oiled grill plate (or grill or barbecue) until browned both sides and puffed slightly.

serves 8
per serving 37.4g fat; 3289kJ (787 cal)
tip Pass each roti over a naked flame just before serving to make it puff and become more supple.

osso buco

PREPARATION TIME 20 MINUTES   COOKING TIME 1 HOUR 45 MINUTES

$^1/_4$ cup (35g) plain flour

8 pieces veal shin or
   osso buco (1kg)

2 tablespoons olive oil

3 large egg tomatoes (270g),
   peeled, chopped coarsely

$^1/_2$ cup (125ml) dry white wine

2 cloves garlic, crushed

2 cups (500ml) chicken stock

POLENTA

1.5 litres (6 cups) water

2 teaspoons salt

$1^1/_2$ cups (250g) polenta

$^1/_2$ cup (125ml) milk

GREMOLATA

$^1/_4$ cup finely chopped fresh
   flat-leaf parsley

2 teaspoons finely chopped
   lemon rind

2 cloves garlic, chopped finely

1 Preheat oven to moderately slow.

2 Place flour in plastic bag. Add one piece of veal at a time, gently shaking bag to coat veal all over. Remove veal from bag, shaking off excess flour; repeat with remaining veal pieces.

3 Heat oil in large flameproof casserole dish over high heat. Cook veal, in batches, until browned on both sides.

4 Return all pieces of veal to dish, fitting them upright and tightly together in a single layer. Add tomato, wine, garlic and stock; if necessary, add enough water so that the liquid just covers the surface of the veal. Bring to a boil; place a round piece of baking paper, cut to the same diameter as the dish, on top of veal. Cover dish with a tight-fitting lid; cook in moderately slow oven 1½ hours.

5 After 1 hour, check liquid content in dish; if it looks too thin, remove dish from oven. Simmer, uncovered, on top of stove until mixture reduces and thickens slightly. Return covered pan to oven; cook osso buco 30 minutes.

6 Divide polenta among serving plates. Top with osso buco; sprinkle with gremolata.

polenta Combine the water and salt in large saucepan over high heat. Bring to a boil; add polenta in a slow, steady stream, stirring constantly; reduce heat to a simmer and cook polenta, uncovered, stirring constantly, about 20 minutes or until polenta is just thickened. Stir in milk; cook, stirring constantly, about 10 minutes or until polenta is thick and creamy.

gremolata Combine ingredients in small bowl; cover tightly with plastic wrap. Refrigerate until required.

serves 4

per serving 14.6g fat; 2710kJ (648 cal)

tips 400g canned undrained tomato pieces can be substituted for the fresh tomato. Recipe can be made a day ahead and refrigerated, covered; suitable to freeze.

slow-cooked lamb shoulder

PREPARATION TIME **15 MINUTES**   COOKING TIME **4 HOURS 15 MINUTES**

2 tablespoons olive oil
1.2kg lamb shoulder
**2 medium brown onions (300g),
   chopped coarsely**
**2 medium carrots (240g),
   chopped coarsely**
**2 trimmed sticks celery (150g),
   chopped coarsely**
1 tablespoon sugar
¹/₂ cup (125ml) dry red wine
¹/₂ cup (125ml) lamb stock
10 sprigs fresh oregano

1 Preheat oven to slow.

2 Heat oil in large flameproof baking dish. Cook lamb, uncovered, over high heat until browned all over; remove lamb from dish. Cook vegetables in same dish, stirring, until browned lightly. Add sugar; cook, stirring, 1 minute. Add wine and stock. Bring to a boil; remove from heat.

3 Place half of the oregano on vegetables; place lamb on top, then place remaining oregano on lamb. Bake, covered tightly, in slow oven 1½ hours. Turn lamb; bake, covered, another 1½ hours. Turn again; bake, covered, further 1 hour.

4 Carefully remove lamb from dish; wrap in foil. Strain pan contents, discarding vegetables, oregano and as much fat as possible. Serve lamb with strained hot juice.

serves 4
per serving 26.4g fat; 2340kJ (559 cal)
tip Beef stock can be substituted for lamb stock, and rosemary can be substituted for oregano.

chilli marinated beef in coconut curry sauce

PREPARATION TIME **20 MINUTES (plus marinating time)**   COOKING TIME **2 HOURS**

1.5kg beef chuck steak, chopped coarsely
40g ghee
2 medium red capsicums (400g), chopped finely
2 medium brown onions (300g), chopped finely
$^1/_2$ cup (125ml) beef stock
$^1/_2$ cup (125ml) coconut milk
1 cinnamon stick
5 dried curry leaves
$^1/_3$ cup chopped fresh coriander

MARINADE
$^1/_3$ cup (80ml) white vinegar
2 fresh red thai chillies, sliced thinly
2 tablespoons tomato paste
1 tablespoon chopped fresh coriander
2 cloves garlic, crushed
3 cardamom pods, crushed
2 teaspoons cumin seeds
1 teaspoon ground turmeric

1   Combine beef and marinade in large bowl; mix well. Cover; refrigerate 3 hours or overnight.
2   Heat half of the ghee in large saucepan; cook beef, in batches, stirring, until browned.
3   Heat remaining ghee in same pan; cook capsicum and onion, stirring, until onion is soft.
4   Return beef to pan; add stock, coconut milk, cinnamon and curry leaves. Simmer, covered, 1 hour, stirring occasionally.
5   Remove cover; simmer about 30 minutes or until beef is tender. Discard cinnamon stick; stir in coriander.
6   Serve with steamed or boiled rice, if desired.

marinade Combine ingredients in large bowl; mix well.

serves 6
per serving 23g fat; 1853kJ (443 cal)
tip Recipe can be made a day ahead and refrigerated, covered; suitable to freeze.

braised beef curry with dhal

PREPARATION TIME **15 MINUTES** (plus refrigeration time)   COOKING TIME **2 HOURS 30 MINUTES**

1 tablespoon peanut oil
2 medium brown onions (300g),
    chopped coarsely
2 cloves garlic, crushed
1 fresh red thai chilli, chopped finely
1 tablespoon grated fresh ginger
2 teaspoons garam masala
2 tablespoons ground cumin
2 tablespoons ground coriander
2 teaspoons hot paprika
4 cardamom pods, bruised
3 cinnamon sticks, broken
2 cups (500ml) water
2kg beef chuck steak, cut into
    2cm pieces
3 cups (750ml) beef stock
½ cup (125ml) coconut milk
⅓ cup chopped fresh coriander
3 cups (600g) red lentils

1 Heat oil in large heavy-base saucepan; cook onion, garlic, chilli and ginger, stirring, until onion is soft. Stir in spices; cook, stirring, until fragrant.
2 Gradually stir ¼ cup (60ml) of the water into onion mixture until it forms a paste; cook, stirring, 2 minutes. Add beef; stir to coat in paste.
3 Add the remaining water and stock; bring to a boil. Reduce heat; simmer, covered, stirring occasionally, about 1½ hours or until beef is tender. Refrigerate overnight, to allow flavours to develop.
4 Add coconut milk; simmer, uncovered, about 30 minutes or until thickened slightly. Discard cardamom pods and cinnamon sticks. Stir in coriander.
5 Meanwhile, cook lentils in medium saucepan of boiling water, uncovered, about 10 minutes or until tender; drain. Serve lentils with curry.

serves 8
per serving 20.1g fat; 2516kJ (602 cal)

braised lamb and yogurt

PREPARATION TIME **20 MINUTES (plus marinating time)**   COOKING TIME **1 HOUR 15 MINUTES**

1 **medium brown onion (150g),**
   chopped coarsely
1 **tablespoon grated fresh ginger**
2 **cloves garlic, crushed**
1 **teaspoon coriander seeds**
1 **teaspoon cumin seeds**
$^1/_2$ **teaspoon cardamom seeds**
2 **tablespoons lime juice**
2.5kg **leg of lamb, boned,**
   chopped coarsely
30g **ghee**
$^1/_4$ **teaspoon cayenne pepper**
2 **teaspoons ground turmeric**
1 **teaspoon garam masala**
$^2/_3$ **cup (190g) plain yogurt**
$^2/_3$ **cup (160ml) cream**
1 **cup (250ml) water**
400g **can chickpeas, rinsed, drained**
2 **medium tomatoes (380g),**
   chopped coarsely
1 **tablespoon plain flour**
2 **tablespoons water, extra**
$^1/_4$ **cup chopped fresh**
   flat-leaf parsley

1   Blend or process onion, ginger, garlic, seeds and juice until well combined. Place blended mixture and lamb in medium bowl; stir until lamb is well coated. Cover; marinate in refrigerator 3 hours or overnight.

2   Heat ghee in large saucepan; add cayenne pepper, turmeric and garam masala; stir over medium heat 1 minute.

3   Stir in yogurt, then lamb; stir over high heat until lamb is well browned. Stir in combined cream and water; bring to a boil. Reduce heat; simmer, uncovered, about 1 hour or until lamb is tender. Stir in chickpeas and tomato.

4   Stir in blended flour and the extra water; stir over high heat until sauce boils and thickens. Stir in parsley; serve with lime wedges, if desired.

serves 6
per serving 37.5g fat; 2877kJ (687 cal)
tips Ask your butcher to bone the leg of lamb for you.
Recipe can be made a day ahead and refrigerated, covered.

barbecue

Perfectly suited to a relaxed style of eating and entertaining, barbecue is the definitive casual food, from the Asian-influenced lime chicken on lemon grass skewers to the hearty flavours of veal T-bone with buttered spinach and roast tomatoes.

salmon with grilled corn salsa

PREPARATION TIME **20 MINUTES**   COOKING TIME **25 MINUTES**

6 salmon fillets or cutlets (1.2kg)

CORN SALSA
2 trimmed corn cobs (500g)
2 medium red capsicums (400g)
1 small red onion (100g),
   chopped finely
1 fresh red thai chilli, seeded,
   chopped finely
1 tablespoon olive oil
¼ cup chopped fresh coriander

1 Cook salmon on heated oiled barbecue plate until browned both sides and cooked as desired. Salmon is best served a little rare in the centre.
2 Serve salmon with corn salsa and grilled bread, if desired.

corn salsa Cook corn on heated oiled barbecue plate, covered loosely with a piece of foil, about 20 minutes or until browned all over and tender. Using a sharp knife, cut kernels from cobs. Quarter capsicums; remove and discard seeds and membranes. Cook on heated oiled barbecue plate until skin blisters and blackens. Cover capsicum pieces with plastic or paper 5 minutes. Peel away and discard skin; chop capsicum flesh finely. Combine corn, capsicum, onion, chilli, oil and coriander in medium bowl.

serves 6
per serving 18.5g fat; 1766kJ (422 cal)
tips Barbecuing corn gives it a distinctive smoky flavour. Corn salsa can be made 3 hours ahead.

vegetable kebabs with balsamic dressing

PREPARATION TIME 20 MINUTES   COOKING TIME 20 MINUTES

250g cherry tomatoes
1 large green capsicum (350g),
   chopped coarsely
6 small flat mushrooms
   (600g), quartered
6 yellow patty-pan squash
   (240g), halved
3 baby eggplant (180g), sliced thickly
3 small zucchini (270g), sliced thickly
1 medium brown onion (150g),
   sliced thickly
500g haloumi cheese, cubed
60g baby rocket leaves

BALSAMIC DRESSING
¹/₃ cup (80ml) olive oil
¹/₄ cup (60ml) balsamic vinegar
1 teaspoon sugar

1 Thread tomatoes, vegetables and cheese onto 12 skewers.
2 Cook kebabs, in batches, on heated oiled barbecue plate until
   browned all over.
3 Serve kebabs on rocket leaves drizzled with balsamic dressing.

balsamic dressing Combine ingredients in screw-top jar; shake well.

serves 4
per serving 40.8g fat; 2402kJ (575 cal)
tip You will need to soak 12 bamboo skewers in water for at least an
hour before use, to prevent them from splintering and scorching.

swordfish with thai dressing

PREPARATION TIME **5 MINUTES**   COOKING TIME **10 MINUTES**

4 swordfish steaks (720g)

THAI DRESSING
$^1/_3$ cup (80ml) sweet chilli sauce
$^1/_2$ cup (125ml) lime juice
1 tablespoon fish sauce
2 teaspoons finely chopped lemon grass
2 tablespoons chopped fresh coriander
$^1/_2$ cup chopped fresh mint
1 teaspoon grated fresh ginger

1 Cook fish on heated oiled barbecue plate until browned
    both sides and cooked as desired.
2 Drizzle thai dressing over fish; serve with mixed salad leaves
    and lemon, if desired.

thai dressing Combine ingredients in screw-top jar; shake well.

serves 4
per serving 4.7g fat; 918kJ (219 cal)
tip This recipe is best made just before serving.

tandoori chicken

PREPARATION TIME **10 MINUTES (plus marinating time)** COOKING TIME **15 MINUTES**

¹/₂ **cup (140g) low-fat plain yogurt**
1 tablespoon lemon juice
¹/₂ **teaspoon finely grated fresh ginger**
1 clove garlic, crushed
¹/₂ **teaspoon caster sugar**
¹/₂ **teaspoon paprika**
¹/₄ **teaspoon ground cumin**
¹/₄ **teaspoon ground coriander**
¹/₄ **teaspoon ground turmeric**
pinch chilli powder
2 x 200g single chicken breast fillets

TOMATO AND CORIANDER SALSA
1 small tomato (130g), chopped finely
¹/₂ **small red onion (50g), chopped finely**
1 teaspoon sugar
1 tablespoon chopped fresh coriander

1 Combine yogurt, juice, ginger, garlic, sugar, paprika and spices in large bowl. Add chicken; turn to coat in marinade. Refrigerate 3 hours or overnight.
2 Cook chicken on heated oiled grill plate, brushing with marinade, until browned both sides and tender. Serve chicken sliced thickly, with tomato and coriander salsa, and steamed rice, if desired.

tomato and coriander salsa Combine ingredients in small bowl.

serves 2
per serving 12.5g fat; 1457kJ (349 cal)
tip Chicken is best marinated a day ahead and refrigerated, covered.

herbed swordfish kebabs

PREPARATION TIME 30 MINUTES (plus marinating time) COOKING TIME 15 MINUTES

2kg swordfish steaks
4 medium lemons (560g)
¹/₃ cup chopped fresh coriander
¹/₂ cup chopped fresh flat-leaf parsley
¹/₂ cup chopped fresh chives
¹/₂ teaspoon freshly ground black pepper
2 tablespoons peanut oil

1 Remove and discard skin from fish; cut fish into 3cm pieces.
2 Using zester, remove as much of the rind as possible from lemons. Squeeze ⅔ cup (160ml) juice from the lemons.
3 Combine fish in large bowl with rind, juice, herbs, pepper and oil; toss to mix well.
4 Thread fish onto 16 skewers; place, in single layer, in large shallow dish. Pour any remaining marinade over skewers. Cover; refrigerate 3 hours or overnight. Cook skewers on heated oiled barbecue plate until browned all over and cooked through. Serve with baby spinach leaves, if desired.

serves 8
per serving 11.8g fat; 1346kJ (322 cal)
tip You will need to soak 16 bamboo skewers in water for at least an hour before use, to prevent them from splintering and scorching.

veal T-bone with buttered spinach and roast tomatoes

PREPARATION TIME **15 MINUTES**   COOKING TIME **1 HOUR**

12 small tomatoes on vine (1.5kg)
4 veal T-bone steaks (850g)
50g butter
2 cloves garlic, crushed
900g spinach, trimmed
$^1/_4$ cup shredded fresh basil leaves
2 tablespoons olive oil
50g pecorino cheese, shaved

1 Preheat oven to moderately slow.
2 Place tomatoes in large oiled baking dish. Roast, uncovered, in moderately slow oven about 1 hour or until tomatoes soften.
3 Meanwhile, cook veal on heated oiled barbecue plate until browned both sides and cooked as desired.
4 Melt butter in large saucepan; cook garlic and spinach until spinach just wilts.
5 Serve veal with spinach and tomatoes. Spoon over combined basil and oil; sprinkle with cheese.

serves 4
per serving 26g fat; 1804kJ (432 cal)

barbecued mixed vegetables

PREPARATION TIME 15 MINUTES   COOKING TIME 20 MINUTES

1 large kumara (500g), sliced thickly
2 large red onions (600g)
¹⁄₂ cup (125ml) olive oil
3 medium red capsicums (600g),
  quartered, seeded
3 medium yellow capsicums (600g),
  quartered, seeded
6 medium zucchini (720g),
  sliced thickly
400g swiss brown mushrooms

1 Boil, steam or microwave kumara until almost tender; drain. Cut each onion into 12 wedges, leaving the root end intact.
2 Cook kumara and onion on heated oiled barbecue plate, brushing with oil, until browned on one side; turn vegetables and repeat.
3 Cook capsicum, zucchini and mushrooms on heated oiled barbecue plate, brushing with oil, until browned and tender.

serves 10
per serving 11.9g fat; 789kJ (189 cal)
tip This recipe is best made just before serving.

lime chicken on lemon grass skewers

PREPARATION TIME **20 MINUTES (plus marinating time)** COOKING TIME **15 MINUTES**

6 x 30cm-long fresh lemon grass stalks
¹/₃ cup (80ml) peanut oil
1 tablespoon grated lime rind
¹/₄ cup chopped fresh coriander
6 single chicken breast fillets (1kg)
¹/₄ cup (60ml) lime juice
2 fresh red thai chillies, seeded,
   chopped finely
¹/₃ cup (80ml) macadamia oil
1 tablespoon raw sugar
1 clove garlic, crushed

1 Cut 3cm off the end of each lemon grass stalk; reserve stalks. Chop the 3cm pieces finely; combine in large shallow dish with peanut oil, rind and coriander.

2 Cut each chicken fillet into three strips crossways; thread three strips onto each lemon grass stalk "skewer". Place skewers in dish with lemon grass marinade; turn skewers to coat chicken in marinade. Cover; refrigerate 3 hours or overnight.

3 Cook skewers on heated oiled barbecue, uncovered, until chicken is browned all over and tender. Meanwhile, combine remaining ingredients in screw-top jar; shake well. Serve with chicken skewers.

serves 6
per serving 33.6g fat; 1907kJ (456 cal)

yakitori chicken

PREPARATION TIME **15 MINUTES**   COOKING TIME **10 MINUTES**

Yakitori is a popular Japanese snack – tiny skewers of grilled chicken pieces, served with a dipping sauce, are consumed with sake after a hard day at the office by thousands of executives! Sometimes accompanied by mushrooms, capsicum strips, onion wedges or quail eggs, the skewers can be threaded with chicken breast or thigh fillet, chicken liver or even minced chicken gizzards.

1kg chicken breast fillets
$1/4$ cup (60ml) mirin
$1/2$ cup (125ml) light soy sauce
2 teaspoons grated fresh ginger
2 cloves garlic, crushed
$1/4$ teaspoon freshly ground black pepper
1 tablespoon sugar

1 Cut chicken into 2cm pieces.
2 Combine chicken with remaining ingredients in large bowl. Drain chicken over small bowl; reserve marinade.
3 Thread chicken onto 12 bamboo skewers. Cook skewers on heated oiled barbecue plate, turning and brushing occasionally with reserved marinade during cooking, until chicken is browned all over and cooked through.

serves 4
per serving   13.8g fat; 1614kJ (386 cal)
tips   Mirin is a somewhat sweet rice wine used in many Asian, especially Japanese, dishes. You can substitute sherry or sweet white wine for mirin, if you prefer.
You will need to soak 12 bamboo skewers in water for at least an hour before use, to prevent them from splintering and scorching.

cumin fish cutlets with coriander chilli sauce

PREPARATION TIME 15 MINUTES   COOKING TIME 10 MINUTES

6 firm white fish cutlets (1.2kg)
2 teaspoons cumin seeds

CORIANDER CHILLI SAUCE
8 green onions, chopped coarsely
3 cloves garlic, crushed
3 fresh red thai chillies, seeded, chopped finely
1 tablespoon finely chopped coriander root
2 tablespoons brown sugar
2 tablespoons fish sauce
¹/₄ cup (60ml) lime juice

1 Sprinkle one side of each cutlet with seeds. Cook fish on heated oiled barbecue plate, until browned on both sides and just cooked through.
2 Serve fish with coriander chilli sauce and lime, if desired.

coriander chilli sauce Using the "pulse" button, blend or process onion, garlic, chilli, coriander root and sugar until chopped finely. Add sauce and juice; blend until combined.

serves 6
per serving 4.3g fat; 915kJ (218 cal)
tip This recipe is best made just before serving.

chicken tikka with cucumber-mint raita

PREPARATION TIME **15 MINUTES** COOKING TIME **10 MINUTES**

The word tikka actually refers to a bite-size piece of meat, poultry, fish or vegetable. Our recipe, a quick version of the popular starter in many Indian restaurants, uses ready-made tikka paste, found in jars in most supermarkets.

1kg chicken breast fillets
¹/₂ cup (150g) tikka paste

CUCUMBER-MINT RAITA
³/₄ cup (200g) yogurt
1 lebanese cucumber (130g), peeled, seeded, chopped finely
2 tablespoons chopped fresh mint
1 teaspoon ground cumin

1 Combine chicken with paste in large bowl.
2 Cook chicken, in batches, on heated oiled barbecue plate until browned all over and cooked through.
3 Serve sliced chicken with cucumber-mint raita on a bed of cabbage with mango chutney, if desired.

cucumber-mint raita Combine ingredients in small bowl.

serves 4
per serving 31.6g fat; 2148kJ (514 cal)
tip You can also serve this recipe in the traditional manner, by threading the chopped or sliced chicken breast fillets onto bamboo skewers before grilling or barbecuing. You will need to soak 12 bamboo skewers in water for at least an hour before use, to prevent them from splintering and scorching.

watermelon and strawberry ice-block

PREPARATION TIME 10 MINUTES (plus freezing time)
COOKING TIME 5 MINUTES (plus cooling time)

⅓ cup (80ml) water
2 tablespoons sugar
250g piece watermelon, peeled, seeded, chopped coarsely
80g strawberries, chopped coarsely
2 teaspoons lemon juice

1 Combine the water and sugar in small saucepan; stir over low heat until sugar dissolves. Bring to a boil; boil, uncovered about 2 minutes or until mixture thickens slightly. Transfer syrup to small bowl; refrigerate until cold.
2 Blend or process cold syrup, watermelon, strawberries and juice until smooth. Pour mixture into four ⅓-cup (80ml) ice-block moulds. Freeze overnight until firm.

serves 4
per serving 0.1g fat; 193kJ (46 cal)

lemonade, lemon and mint ice-block

PREPARATION TIME 5 MINUTES (plus freezing time)

1½ cups (375ml) lemonade
1 teaspoon finely grated lemon rind
1 tablespoon lemon juice
2 teaspoons finely chopped fresh mint

1 Combine ingredients in medium freezerproof jug; freeze mixture about 1 hour or until partially frozen. Stir; pour mixture into four ⅓-cup (80ml) ice-block moulds. Freeze overnight until firm.

serves 4
per serving 0.02g fat; 172kJ (41 cal)

spiced coffee ice-block

PREPARATION TIME 5 MINUTES
(plus cooling and freezing times)

2 teaspoons instant coffee
2 teaspoons drinking chocolate
2 teaspoons caster sugar
¼ teaspoon ground cinnamon
1 tablespoon boiling water
⅔ cup (160ml) cream, whipped lightly

1 Combine coffee, drinking chocolate, sugar and cinnamon in medium jug. Add the water, stirring until sugar dissolves, cool 5 minutes; gently stir in cream. Pour mixture into four ⅓-cup (80ml) ice-block moulds. Freeze overnight until firm.

serves 4
per serving 17.5g fat; 729kJ (174 cal)

honey, banana and yogurt ice-block

PREPARATION TIME 5 MINUTES (plus freezing time)

1 large banana (230g)
⅔ cup (190g) vanilla yogurt
1 tablespoon honey

1 Blend or process ingredients until mixture is smooth and creamy. Pour into four ⅓-cup (80ml) ice-block moulds. Freeze overnight until firm.

serves 4
per serving 1.7g fat; 417kJ (100 cal)

on the side

Accompany any meal with a selection of delicious side dishes –
a plate of crunchy garlic kipfler potatoes, a cool asparagus,
avocado and macadamia salad, or a bowl of steaming hot asian
greens in oyster sauce – and you'll transform a snack into a feast.

buttery mashed celeriac

PREPARATION TIME **15 MINUTES**   COOKING TIME **20 MINUTES**

2kg celeriac, peeled, chopped coarsely
90g butter, chopped
1 tablespoon chopped fresh chives

1 Boil or steam celeriac until tender; drain. Mash celeriac with 80g of the butter until smooth.

2 Serve topped with the remaining butter and chives.

serves 4
per serving 19.3g fat; 1163kJ (278 cal)
tip This recipe can be made a day ahead and refrigerated, covered.

roasted kumara mash

**4 large kumara (2kg),
  chopped coarsely**
2 tablespoons olive oil
1 cup (250ml) buttermilk
20g butter

1 Preheat oven to moderately hot.
2 Combine kumara in large baking dish with oil; cook, uncovered, in moderately hot oven about 1 hour or until kumara is tender.
3 Blend or process kumara with remaining ingredients until pureed. Transfer to medium saucepan; reheat, stirring, until hot.

serves 8
per serving 7.7g fat; 910kJ (218 cal)
tips Make the mash just before serving.
Add a little lemon juice or a few tablespoons of a freshly chopped herb such as thyme, dill or even flat-leaf parsley, if desired.

bok choy steamed with chilli oil

PREPARATION TIME **5 MINUTES**   COOKING TIME **5 MINUTES**

4 baby bok choy (600g)
1 tablespoon peanut oil
2 cloves garlic, crushed
2 tablespoons light soy sauce
1$^1/_2$ teaspoons hot chilli sauce
2 green onions, sliced thinly
$^1/_4$ cup fresh coriander leaves
1 fresh red thai chilli, seeded, sliced thinly

1 Halve bok choy lengthways; place, cut-side up, in bamboo steamer. Drizzle bok choy with combined oil, garlic and sauces.
2 Steam bok choy, covered, over wok or large saucepan of simmering water about 5 minutes or until just tender. Serve bok choy sprinkled with onion, coriander and chilli.

serves 4
per serving 5g fat; 273kJ (65 cal)

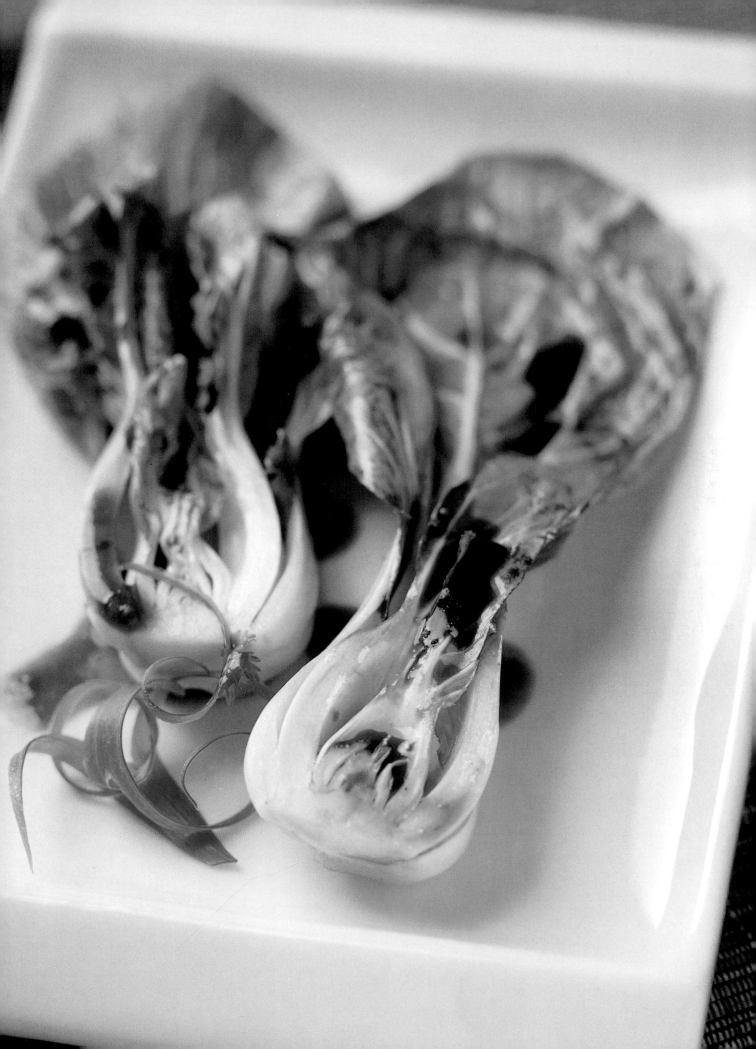

fresh asparagus topped with garlic breadcrumbs and chopped eggs

PREPARATION TIME **10 MINUTES**   COOKING TIME **10 MINUTES**

80g butter
2 tablespoons honey
2 cloves garlic, crushed
1 cup (70g) stale breadcrumbs
1kg fresh asparagus, trimmed
2 hard-boiled eggs, chopped finely
$^1/_3$ cup chopped fresh flat-leaf parsley

1 Melt half of the butter and half of the honey in large frying pan. Add garlic and breadcrumbs; cook, stirring, until breadcrumbs are browned and crisp.
2 Boil, steam or microwave asparagus until just tender; drain.
3 Serve asparagus scattered with breadcrumb mixture, egg and parsley; drizzle with combined remaining melted butter and honey.

serves 8
per serving 9.9g fat; 621kJ (149 cal)
tips This recipe is best made just before serving, so breadcrumbs stay crisp.
One of the easiest ways to dice an egg is to use an egg slice. After slicing in one direction, hold egg and turn at a 90-degree angle; slice a second time, cutting egg into cubes. If you don't have an egg slice, you can use a grater.

beans and sugar snap peas with lemon and capers

PREPARATION TIME **10 MINUTES**   COOKING TIME **10 MINUTES**

300g butter beans
200g sugar snap peas
2 tablespoons drained tiny capers
¼ cup (60ml) lemon juice
2 tablespoons chopped fresh dill

1   Boil, steam or microwave beans and peas, separately, until just tender; drain.
2   Heat large oiled frying pan; cook capers, stirring, until browned lightly. Add juice, beans and peas; stir until vegetables are hot. Stir in dill.

serves 4
per serving 0.6g fat; 167kJ (40 cal)

cauliflower with chilli and pine nuts

PREPARATION TIME **10 MINUTES** COOKING TIME **10 MINUTES**

1 small cauliflower (1kg)
2 tablespoons extra virgin olive oil
2 cloves garlic, crushed
2 tablespoons pine nuts
2 teaspoons chopped dried chilli
2 tablespoons chopped fresh flat-leaf parsley

1 Separate cauliflower into pieces. Boil, steam or microwave cauliflower until almost tender. Drain; pat dry.
2 Heat oil in medium frying pan; cook garlic, pine nuts and chilli, stirring, over low heat until fragrant and nuts are browned lightly.
3 Add cauliflower; cook, stirring, until well coated with oil mixture.
4 Add parsley; stir until combined.

serves 8
per serving 7.5g fat; 385kJ (92 cal)
tip This recipe is best made just before serving.

asian greens in oyster sauce

PREPARATION TIME **10 MINUTES**   COOKING TIME **10 MINUTES**

1 cup (250ml) chicken stock
¹/₃ cup (80ml) oyster sauce
2 teaspoons sesame oil
2kg baby bok choy, trimmed
1kg choy sum, trimmed

1 Combine stock, sauce and oil in wok or large frying pan; bring
to a boil.

2 Add bok choy; cook, stirring, about 3 minutes or until bok choy
is slightly wilted.

3 Stir in choy sum; cook, covered, about 5 minutes or until both
greens are tender and just wilted.

serves 6
per serving 1.9g fat; 211kJ (50 cal)
tip Use any leafy green Asian vegetables you like in this recipe
but be certain that you prepare the recipe just before serving.

garlic kipfler potatoes

PREPARATION TIME **10 MINUTES**   COOKING TIME **55 MINUTES**

1kg kipfler potatoes
8 cloves garlic
1 teaspoon salt

1 Preheat oven to hot.
2 Boil, steam or microwave potatoes until just tender; drain. Cut potatoes in half lengthways; place in oiled baking dish with garlic. Sprinkle with salt.
3 Bake, uncovered, in hot oven about 45 minutes or until potato is brown and crisp. Squeeze two of the roasted garlic cloves over potato; shake gently to combine.

serves 4
per serving 0.4g fat; 706kJ (169 cal)

spicy potato salad

PREPARATION TIME **10 MINUTES**
COOKING TIME **30 MINUTES (plus cooling time)**

6 medium potatoes (1.2kg), chopped coarsely
$1/4$ cup (60ml) peanut oil
1 teaspoon black mustard seeds
1 teaspoon cumin seeds
1 teaspoon ground cumin
$1/2$ teaspoon sweet paprika
$1 1/2$ teaspoons ground turmeric
$1/4$ teaspoon chilli flakes
1 clove garlic, crushed
2 tablespoons lemon juice
$1/4$ cup chopped fresh coriander

1 Preheat oven to hot. Boil, steam or microwave potato until just
   tender; rinse under cold running water. Drain potato; cool.
2 Combine potato, oil, seeds, spices, garlic and juice in baking
   dish. Cook in hot oven about 20 minutes or until potato is brown.
   Top with coriander to serve.

serves 6
per serving 10.2g fat; 960kJ (230 cal)
tip Recipe can be made 3 hours ahead and
refrigerated, covered.

crispy noodle and cabbage salad

PREPARATION TIME 15 MINUTES

3 cups (240g) finely shredded cabbage

3 cups (240g) finely shredded red cabbage

300g packet crunchy noodles

8 green onions, chopped finely

1/2 cup chopped fresh flat-leaf parsley

2 tablespoons sesame seeds, toasted

DRESSING

1 tablespoon sesame oil

1 tablespoon peanut oil

2 tablespoons white vinegar

2 tablespoons light soy sauce

1/2 cup (125ml) sweet chilli sauce

1 Place cabbage, noodles, onion, parsley and seeds in large bowl.

2 Pour over dressing; toss to combine.

dressing Combine ingredients in screw-top jar; shake well.

serves 4

per serving 22.8g fat; 1464kJ (350 cal)

tips Make salad just before serving or the noodles will lose their crispness; either flat or round crunchy noodles can be used in this recipe.

The dressing can be made a day ahead and refrigerated, covered.

asparagus, avocado and macadamia salad

PREPARATION TIME 10 MINUTES
COOKING TIME 5 MINUTES (plus cooling time)

750g asparagus, halved

150g baby rocket leaves

1 large avocado (320g), sliced thinly

1/2 cup (75g) macadamias, toasted, chopped coarsely

2 tablespoons sherry vinegar

1/4 cup (60ml) macadamia (or olive) oil

1 Cook asparagus, in batches, on heated oiled grill plate (or grill or barbecue), until just tender; cool.

2 Combine asparagus on serving platter with rocket, avocado and nuts.

3 Just before serving, drizzle with the combined vinegar and oil.

serves 8

per serving 20.6g fat; 852kJ (204 cal)

tip This recipe can be prepared 3 hours ahead; add the avocado and dressing just before serving.

beetroot and mozzarella salad

PREPARATION TIME 25 MINUTES
COOKING TIME 30 MINUTES (plus cooling time)

2 medium red capsicums (400g)
8 baby red beetroot (200g)
8 baby golden beetroot (200g)
150g mozzarella cheese, chopped coarsely
2 medium oranges (480g), peeled, segmented
2 tablespoons red wine vinegar
1 tablespoon extra virgin olive oil
120g mesclun
8 slices crusty bread, toasted

1 Preheat oven to moderately hot. Quarter capsicums; remove and discard seeds and membranes. Roast in moderately hot oven, skin-side up, until skin blisters and blackens; cover capsicum pieces with plastic or paper 5 minutes. Peel away and discard skin; slice capsicum flesh into wide strips.
2 Remove stems from beetroot; cook beetroot in boiling water about 10 minutes or until tender; cool. Peel beetroot.
3 Combine capsicum, mozzarella, orange, vinegar and oil. Arrange mesclun on serving plates; top with capsicum mixture and beetroot. Serve with toast.

serves 4
per serving 13.6g fat; 2159kJ (517 cal)
tips All red beetroot can be substituted for golden beetroot, and bocconcini can be substituted for mozzarella. Ciabatta, a crusty Italian bread, is ideal for this recipe.

two-tomato salad

PREPARATION TIME 10 MINUTES

400g cherry tomatoes
250g yellow teardrop tomatoes, halved
½ cup baby basil leaves
2 tablespoons balsamic vinegar

1 Combine tomatoes and basil in medium serving bowl. Add vinegar just before serving. Sprinkle with freshly ground black pepper, if desired.

serves 4
per serving 0.2g fat; 93kJ (22 cal)

desserts

Tropical fruit mini pavlovas, crème brulée, berry tiramisu –
these are just a few of the classic recipes you'll find here.
What better way to complete the perfect casual feast
than with a divinely decadent dessert?

vanilla panna cotta with strawberries

PREPARATION TIME **20 MINUTES (plus refrigeration time)**   COOKING TIME **5 MINUTES**

300ml thickened cream
1 cup (250ml) milk
¹⁄₃ cup (75g) caster sugar
2 teaspoons vanilla essence
2¹⁄₂ teaspoons gelatine
1 tablespoon water
250g strawberries, halved
¹⁄₄ cup (60ml) orange juice
2 teaspoons icing sugar mixture

1 Grease six ½-cup (125ml) moulds.
2 Combine cream, milk and sugar in small saucepan; stir over low heat until sugar dissolves. Stir in essence.
3 Sprinkle gelatine over the water in heatproof cup. Stand cup in small saucepan of simmering water; stir until gelatine dissolves.
4 Stir gelatine mixture into cream mixture. Pour evenly into prepared dishes. Cover; refrigerate about 6 hours or until set.
5 Meanwhile, combine strawberries, juice and icing sugar in medium bowl. Cover; refrigerate 1 hour.
6 Just before serving, turn panna cotta onto serving plates; serve with strawberry mixture.

serves 6
per serving 20.1g fat; 1129kJ (270 cal)
tip This recipe can be made a day ahead.

flourless chocolate hazelnut cake

PREPARATION TIME **15 MINUTES**   COOKING TIME **1 HOUR 15 MINUTES** (plus cooling time)

The rich dense hazelnut meal in this recipe is used instead of flour.

$^1/_3$ **cup (35g) cocoa powder**
$^1/_3$ **cup (80ml) hot water**
150g dark chocolate, melted
150g unsalted butter, melted
1$^1/_3$ cups (275g) firmly packed
   brown sugar
1 cup (110g) hazelnut meal
4 eggs, separated

1 Preheat oven to moderate. Grease deep 20cm-round cake pan; line base and side with baking paper.
2 Combine cocoa and the water in large bowl; stir until smooth. Add chocolate, butter, sugar and hazelnut meal; stir until combined. Stir in egg yolks, one at a time, stirring well after each addition.
3 Beat egg whites in small bowl with electric mixer until soft peaks form; fold, in two batches, into chocolate mixture.
4 Pour mixture into prepared pan. Bake in moderate oven about 1¼ hours; cool in pan. Serve with berries and thickened cream, and dusted with sifted cocoa powder, if desired.

serves 8
per serving 32.6g fat; 2068kJ (495 cal)
tip This cake can be made 4 days ahead and refrigerated, covered, or frozen for up to 3 months.

crème brulée

PREPARATION TIME **15 MINUTES (plus refrigeration time)**
COOKING TIME **40 MINUTES**

1 vanilla bean
3 cups (750ml) thickened cream
6 egg yolks
$^1/_4$ cup (55g) caster sugar
$^1/_3$ cup (55g) pure icing sugar, approximately

1 Preheat oven to moderately slow. Split vanilla bean in half lengthways. Using the point of a sharp knife, scrape seeds from bean; reserve seeds. Place bean and cream in medium saucepan; heat until just below boiling point.

2 Meanwhile, whisk egg yolks, caster sugar and vanilla seeds in medium heatproof bowl; gradually whisk in hot cream mixture. Place bowl over medium saucepan of simmering water – do not have the water touching base of bowl. Stir over heat about 10 minutes or until mixture thickens slightly and coats the back of a spoon.

3 Remove bean – it can be washed, dried and kept for another use. Place six ½-cup (125ml) ovenproof dishes in baking dish; pour cream mixture into ovenproof dishes level with the top as they will shrink slightly. Add enough boiling water to baking dish to come ¾ of the way up side of dishes. Bake in moderately slow oven about 20 minutes or until custard is just set. Remove dishes from water; cool to room temperature. Cover; refrigerate 3 hours or overnight.

4 Place dishes in shallow baking dish filled with ice-cubes (the ice helps to keep custard firm while grilling). Sprinkle each custard evenly with a heaped teaspoon of sifted icing sugar; wipe edge of dishes. Place under hot grill until sugar is just melted, not coloured. Sprinkle custards again with a second layer of sifted icing sugar; place under hot grill until sugar is golden brown.

serves 6
per serving 51.6g fat; 2367kJ (566 cal)
tips Alternatively, use a small blow torch to melt and caramelise the sugar.
This recipe can be prepared a day ahead; grill the tops up to an hour before serving.

panettone and butter pudding

PREPARATION TIME 20 MINUTES (plus standing time)   COOKING TIME 1 HOUR 30 MINUTES (plus cooling time)

1kg panettone
90g butter, softened
3 cups (750ml) milk
300ml cream
½ cup (110g) caster sugar
5cm piece vanilla bean
2 egg yolks
3 eggs
¼ cup (80g) apricot jam
1 tablespoon Grand Marnier

1 Preheat oven to moderately slow. Grease deep 22cm-round cake pan; line base and side with baking paper.

2 Cut panettone in half lengthways, reserve half for another use. Cut in half lengthways again, then crossways into 1.5cm slices. Toast panettone lightly both sides; spread one side with butter while still warm.

3 Slightly overlap slices around sides of prepared pan; layer remaining slices in centre.

4 Combine milk, cream, sugar and split vanilla bean in medium saucepan; stir over heat until mixture comes to a boil. Strain into large jug. Cover; cool 10 minutes.

5 Beat egg yolks and eggs in large bowl; gradually beat in milk mixture. Pour custard over bread in pan.

6 Place cake pan in baking dish; add enough boiling water to dish to come halfway up side of pan.

7 Bake, uncovered, about 1¼ hours or until set. Stand pudding in pan 30 minutes before carefully turning out.

8 Combine jam and liqueur in small bowl; brush evenly over warm pudding. Serve with cream and raspberries, if desired.

serves 8
per serving 47.5g fat; 3459kJ (827 cal)
tips Milk mixture suitable to microwave.
Cointreau or boiling water can be substituted for the Grand Marnier.
Panettone is a sweet Italian celebration yeast bread; you can also use fruit bread.
This recipe is best made on day of serving, but will keep up to 2 days.

hazelnut crème caramel

PREPARATION TIME **25 MINUTES (plus standing and refrigeration times)** COOKING TIME **55 MINUTES**

125g hazelnuts
1 cup (250ml) milk
1¹/₂ cups (375ml) cream
³/₄ cup (165g)
caster sugar
³/₄ cup (180ml) water
3 eggs
3 egg yolks
¹/₂ cup (110g) caster
sugar, extra

1 Preheat oven to moderate. Place nuts in lamington pan; bake in moderate oven about 8 minutes or until skins begin to split and nuts are toasted lightly. Place nuts in tea towel; rub vigorously to remove skins. Chop nuts coarsely. Reduce oven temperature to slow.

2 Bring milk, cream and nuts to a boil in medium saucepan; cover. Remove from heat; stand 20 minutes.

3 Meanwhile, combine sugar and the water in medium saucepan; stir over low heat, without boiling, until sugar dissolves. Brush down side of pan with pastry brush dipped in water to remove any sugar grains. Bring to a boil; boil, uncovered, without stirring, until mixture is caramel in colour. Remove from heat; divide between six ³/₄-cup (180ml) ovenproof moulds. The toffee will set immediately.

4 Combine eggs, egg yolks and extra sugar in medium bowl; whisk until just combined. Bring milk and cream back to a boil; gradually whisk into egg mixture until combined. Strain mixture into large jug; discard nuts.

5 Pour custard over toffee in moulds; place moulds into baking dish. Pour enough boiling water into baking dish to come ³/₄ of the way up side of moulds.

6 Bake, uncovered, in slow oven 35 minutes. Custards are ready when only the centre has a slight wobble to it. Remove from baking dish; refrigerate at least 8 hours or overnight before serving. The refrigeration time allows the toffee to dissolve, which forms the sauce.

7 Gently pull custard away from side of moulds. Invert onto serving plates.

serves 6
per serving 47.2g fat; 2738kJ (654 cal)
tips Cream mixture suitable to microwave.
This recipe is best made a day ahead.

plum clafouti

PREPARATION TIME **15 MINUTES**   COOKING TIME **40 MINUTES**

1^1/$_2$ cups (375ml) low-fat custard
^{1}/$_4$ cup (35g) self-raising flour
1 egg yolk
2 egg whites
825g can whole plums, drained, halved, seeded
2 teaspoons icing sugar mixture

1 Preheat oven to moderate.
2 Combine custard, flour and egg yolk in medium bowl.
3 Beat egg whites in small bowl of electric mixer on highest speed until soft peaks form; fold gently into custard mixture. Pour into 24cm-round ovenproof pie dish.
4 Pat plums dry with absorbent paper; arrange plums, cut-side down, over custard. Place pie dish on oven tray.
5 Bake in moderate oven, uncovered, about 40 minutes or until firm.
6 Just before serving, dust with sifted icing sugar. Serve with vanilla ice-cream, if desired.

serves 4
per serving 2.6g fat; 1019kJ (244 cal)
tip Canned apricots or peaches can be substituted for the plums.

walnut and raisin loaf with brie

PREPARATION TIME **10 MINUTES**   COOKING TIME **35 MINUTES** (plus cooling time)

$^1/_3$ **cup (55g) raisins**
90g butter
$^1/_2$ **cup (100g) firmly packed
    brown sugar**
$^1/_3$ **cup (80ml) water**
$^1/_2$ **teaspoon bicarbonate of soda**
2 eggs, beaten lightly
$^1/_2$ **cup (60g) chopped walnuts**
$^1/_2$ **cup (75g) plain flour**
$^1/_2$ **cup (75g) self-raising flour**
200g brie cheese
1 large bunch grapes (550g)

1   Combine raisins, butter, sugar and the water in medium saucepan; bring to a boil. Remove from heat; stir in soda. Transfer to medium bowl; cool 15 minutes.
2   Preheat oven to slow. Grease 8cm x 25cm bar cake pan; line base with baking paper.
3   Stir egg and nuts into raisin mixture; stir in sifted flours. Pour mixture into prepared pan. Bake in slow oven about 35 minutes or until cooked when tested by inserting a metal skewer into the loaf. Turn onto wire rack to cool.
4   Serve sliced with brie and grapes.

serves 8
per serving 23.3g fat; 1566kJ (374 cal)
tip This recipe can be made a day ahead and is suitable to freeze.

berry tiramisu

PREPARATION TIME **15 MINUTES** (plus refrigeration time)

1³/₄ cups (430ml) thickened cream
¹/₄ cup (40g) icing sugar mixture
1 teaspoon finely grated orange rind
250g mascarpone
¹/₄ cup (60ml) Cointreau
150g blueberries
240g raspberries
250g strawberries, quartered
1 cup (250ml) fresh orange juice
20 sponge finger biscuits (300g)

1 Beat cream, sugar and rind in small bowl, with electric mixer, until soft peaks form; fold in mascarpone and 2 teaspoons of the liqueur.
2 Combine berries and another 2 teaspoons of the liqueur in medium bowl.
3 Combine remaining liqueur and juice in medium bowl. Soak sponge fingers, one at a time, in juice mixture 30 seconds. Arrange half of the sponge fingers around base of 8-cup (2-litre) serving dish. Top with half of the cream mixture; sprinkle with half of the berry mixture.
4 Layer remaining sponge fingers over berries. Repeat cream and berry layers. Cover; refrigerate 6 hours or overnight.

serves 8
per serving 39.8g fat; 2298kJ (549 cal)
tip This recipe can be made a day ahead.

hot passionfruit soufflés

PREPARATION TIME 7 MINUTES   COOKING TIME 10 MINUTES

1 tablespoon caster sugar
2 egg yolks
$\frac{1}{2}$ cup (125ml) passionfruit pulp
1 teaspoon finely grated lemon rind
$\frac{1}{2}$ cup (80g) icing sugar mixture
4 egg whites

1 Preheat oven to moderately hot. Grease six ¾-cup (180ml) ovenproof soufflé dishes. Sprinkle bases and sides evenly with caster sugar; shake away excess. Place dishes on oven tray.

2 Whisk egg yolks in medium bowl with passionfruit, rind and two tablespoons of the sifted icing sugar, until combined.

3 Beat egg whites in small bowl with electric mixer until soft peaks form. Add remaining sifted icing sugar; continue beating until firm peaks form. Fold a quarter of the egg white mixture into passionfruit mixture; gently fold in remaining egg white mixture.

4 Spoon into prepared dishes; bake in moderately hot oven about 10 minutes or until soufflés are well risen and browned.

5 Dust tops with extra sifted icing sugar, if desired.

serves 6
per serving 3.6g fat; 504kJ (120 cal)
tips You will need six passionfruit for this recipe.
The soufflés must be made just before serving.

rich chocolate meringue cake

PREPARATION TIME 15 MINUTES   COOKING TIME 1 HOUR 30 MINUTES (plus cooling time)

8 egg whites
1 cup (220g) caster sugar
¹/₄ cup (25g) cocoa powder
60g dark chocolate, chopped finely
¹/₄ cup (60g) glacé figs, chopped finely
¹/₄ cup (60g) prunes, chopped finely
³/₄ cup (50g) stale breadcrumbs
1 tablespoon icing sugar mixture
1 tablespoon cocoa powder, extra

1   Preheat oven to very slow. Grease 22cm springform pan; line base with baking paper. Flour side of pan; shake away excess.

2   Beat egg whites in large bowl with electric mixer until soft peaks form. Gradually add caster sugar; beat until sugar dissolves between additions.

3   Fold in sifted cocoa, chocolate, fruit and breadcrumbs. Spoon mixture into prepared pan. Bake in very slow oven about 1½ hours or until firm; cool in oven with door ajar.

4   Dust cake with sifted icing sugar and extra cocoa.

serves 8
per serving   2.6g fat; 944kJ (226 cal)
tip   This recipe can be made 2 days ahead.

warm lemon meringue pots

PREPARATION TIME 20 MINUTES   COOKING TIME 15 MINUTES

2 tablespoons cornflour
¹⁄₂ cup (110g) caster sugar
¹⁄₄ cup (60ml) lemon juice
¹⁄₂ cup (125ml) water
1 teaspoon finely grated lemon rind
2 eggs, separated
30g butter, chopped
2 tablespoons thickened cream
¹⁄₃ cup (75g) caster sugar, extra

1 Preheat oven to moderately hot.

2 Combine cornflour and sugar in small saucepan. Gradually add juice and the water; stir until smooth. Cook, stirring constantly, until mixture boils and thickens. Reduce heat; simmer, stirring, 1 minute. Remove from heat; stir in rind, egg yolks, butter and cream.

3 Divide mixture between four ½-cup (125ml) ovenproof dishes. Place dishes onto oven tray.

4 Beat egg whites in small bowl with electric mixer until soft peaks form. Gradually beat in extra caster sugar until dissolved.

5 Spoon meringue over filling. Bake in moderately hot oven about 5 minutes or until browned lightly. Serve with sponge finger biscuits, if desired.

serves 4
per serving 12.4g fat; 1347kJ (322 cal)
tip This recipe is best made just before serving.

summer berry and almond tart

PREPARATION TIME 30 MINUTES (plus refrigeration time)
COOKING TIME 50 MINUTES (plus cooling time)

1^2/$_3$ cups (250g) plain flour
^{1}/$_3$ cup (55g) icing sugar mixture
2 teaspoons grated orange rind
150g cold butter, chopped
1 egg
350g fresh mixed berries

FILLING
90g butter
1 teaspoon vanilla essence
^{1}/$_2$ cup (110g) caster sugar
1 egg
1 tablespoon plain flour
1 cup (100g) almond meal

1 Process flour, icing sugar, rind and butter until combined. Add egg; process until pastry just comes together.
2 Shape pastry into round. Cover; refrigerate 1 hour.
3 Roll pastry between two sheets of baking paper until large enough to line base and side of 26cm-round loose-base flan tin. Ease pastry into tin, pressing lightly into side. Trim edge with sharp knife or rolling pin. Place tin on oven tray; refrigerate 15 minutes.
4 Preheat oven to moderate. Cover pastry with baking paper; fill with dried beans or rice. Bake in moderate oven 10 minutes. Remove paper and beans. Bake further 5 minutes or until pastry is golden brown; cool.
5 Spoon filling into pastry base; scatter berries over filling. Bake in moderate oven 35 minutes or until filling is golden and firm; cool.
6 Serve with whipped cream and dusted with icing sugar, if desired.

filling Beat butter, vanilla and sugar in small bowl with electric mixer until pale. Beat in egg until combined; stir in flour and almond meal.

serves 8
per serving 33.3g fat; 2144kJ (512 cal)
tips Pastry suitable to freeze.
This recipe can be made a day ahead.

mango sorbet

PREPARATION TIME **20 MINUTES (plus freezing time)**   COOKING TIME **8 MINUTES (plus cooling time)**

1 cup (220g) sugar
1 cup (250ml) water
⅓ cup (80ml) lemon juice
4 medium mangoes (1.7kg), peeled,
    chopped coarsely
2 egg whites, beaten lightly

1 Combine sugar and the water in medium saucepan. Stir over medium heat, without boiling, until sugar dissolves; add juice. Bring to a boil; reduce heat. Simmer, uncovered, 5 minutes; cool.

2 Blend or process mango until smooth. Add lemon syrup; process until combined. Stir in egg whites.

3 Pour mixture into freezerproof container. Cover; freeze until sorbet is just firm. Chop sorbet; process mixture until smooth. Return sorbet to container. Cover; freeze until firm.

serves 6
per serving 0.4g fat; 1097kJ (262 cal)
tips For best results use fresh mango. You will need about 3½ cups mango puree for this recipe. Mango sorbet can be made a week ahead.
Sorbet can also be made using an ice-cream maker, following manufacturer's instructions.

tropical fruit mini pavlovas

PREPARATION TIME 20 MINUTES   COOKING TIME 45 MINUTES (plus cooling time)

6 egg whites
1¹/₂ cups (330g) caster sugar
300ml thickened cream
1 medium kiwi fruit (85g), peeled,
   halved, sliced thinly
1 small mango (300g), peeled,
   sliced thinly
2 passionfruit
shaved fresh coconut

1 Preheat oven to very slow. Draw eight 8.5cm circles on a large sheet of baking paper. Grease oven tray; place paper, pencil side down, on tray.
2 Beat egg whites in large bowl with electric mixer until soft peaks form. Gradually add sugar; continue beating about 10 minutes or until sugar dissolves.
3 Divide mixture evenly among circles; shape using a palette knife. Bake in very slow oven about 45 minutes or until crisp and dry. Cool pavlovas in oven with door ajar.
4 Beat cream in small bowl with electric mixer until soft peaks form.
5 Just before serving, top pavlovas with cream, fruit and coconut.

serves 8
per serving 14.8g fat; 1402kJ (335 cal)
tips To open a fresh coconut, pierce the "eyes" with a strong metal skewer; drain liquid. Place coconut on ground and hit sharply with a hammer. Remove outer husk. Use vegetable peeler to shave flakes; flaked dry coconut can be substituted.
Pavlova shells can be made 3 days ahead and stored in an airtight container in a cool, dry place. Add cream and fruit just before serving.

chocolate nougat frozen parfait

PREPARATION TIME **20 MINUTES** (plus freezing time)

2 cups (400g) ricotta cheese
¹/₂ cup (110g) caster sugar
300ml thickened cream
200g dark chocolate, melted
150g almond nougat, chopped finely

1 Line base and two long sides of 14cm x 21cm loaf pan with foil or baking paper, extending over edge of sides.
2 Blend or process ricotta and sugar until smooth; transfer to medium bowl. Beat cream in small bowl with electric mixer until soft peaks form. Fold cream into ricotta mixture; fold in chocolate and nougat.
3 Spoon mixture into prepared pan. Cover with foil; freeze overnight or until firm.
4 Turn out of pan; cut into slices. Stand 10 minutes before serving, to allow it to soften slightly.
5 Serve sliced with raspberries, if desired.

serves 6
per serving 37.6g fat; 2540kJ (607 cal)
tips Chocolate suitable to microwave.
This recipe is best made a day ahead.

coconut and vanilla parfait

PREPARATION TIME 10 MINUTES

⅓ cup (80ml) coconut cream
1.5 litres vanilla ice-cream, softened
2 tablespoons passionfruit pulp
⅓ cup (15g) flaked coconut, toasted

1 Combine coconut cream and ice-cream in large bowl. Divide mixture evenly between four parfait glasses. Top each parfait with passionfruit pulp and coconut.

serves 4
per serving 22.9g fat; 1574kJ (376 cal)

marsala and almond mascarpone

PREPARATION TIME 10 MINUTES

250g mascarpone
2 tablespoons marsala
⅓ cup (55g) sugared almonds, chopped coarsely
½ cup (125ml) thickened cream, whipped
1 tablespoon honey
4 sponge finger biscuits

1 Combine mascarpone, marsala, almond, cream and honey in medium bowl. Spoon mascarpone mixture into individual serving glasses. Serve with biscuits.

serves 4
per serving 52.9g fat; 2515kJ (601 cal)

sticky pears

PREPARATION TIME 10 MINUTES
COOKING TIME 7 MINUTES

40g butter
4 medium pears (920g), peeled, halved lengthways
1/3 cup (75g) firmly packed brown sugar
1 teaspoon ground cardamom
2 tablespoons green ginger wine
2/3 cup (160ml) double cream

1 Heat butter in large heavy-base frying pan; cook pear, sugar,
  cardamom and wine over high heat, stirring occasionally,
  about 5 minutes or until pears are browned. Serve hot pears
  with cream.

serves 4
per serving 29.3g fat; 1847kJ (441 cal)

berries with white chocolate sauce

PREPARATION TIME 10 MINUTES
COOKING TIME 5 MINUTES

1/2 cup (125ml) cream
125g white chocolate, chopped finely
1 tablespoon Malibu
500g strawberries, quartered
300g blueberries

1 Bring cream to a boil in medium saucepan; remove from
  heat. Add chocolate; stir until smooth. Stir in liqueur.
  Serve warm sauce over berries.

serves 4
per serving 24.2g fat; 1569kJ (375 cal)

fast desserts

sweet treats

Enjoy scrumptious sweets like these little lime friands with a freshly brewed cup of coffee or a pot of afternoon tea, in fact whenever the mood takes you. Or indulge your chocolate cravings with any of the delicious tarts, truffles, brownies and biscotti featured here.

mocha hazelnut biscotti

PREPARATION TIME 20 MINUTES   COOKING TIME 45 MINUTES (plus cooling time)

1¼ cups (185g) hazelnuts
3 eggs
½ cup (100g) firmly packed
   brown sugar
½ cup (110g) caster sugar
1½ cups (225g) plain flour
1 cup (150g) self-raising flour
⅓ cup (35g) cocoa powder
2 teaspoons instant coffee powder
2 tablespoons Frangelico
100g dark chocolate, grated finely

1 Preheat oven to moderate. Spread nuts in single layer on oven tray; bake in moderate oven about 5 minutes or until the skins begin to split. Rub nuts firmly in clean tea towel to remove skins.

2 Beat eggs and sugars in medium bowl with electric mixer until smooth and changed in colour. Stir in sifted flours and cocoa, combined coffee and liqueur, chocolate and nuts; mix to a firm dough.

3 Gently knead dough on floured surface until smooth; divide dough in half. Shape each half into a 7cm x 20cm log. Place logs on greased large oven tray. Bake, uncovered, in moderate oven about 30 minutes or until firm. Cool on tray 15 minutes.

4 Using a serrated knife, cut logs on an angle into 5mm slices; place slices on oven trays. Bake in moderate oven 15 minutes or until both sides are dry and crisp; cool. Serve with coffee, if desired.

makes 50
per biscotti 3.9g fat; 378kJ (90 cal)
tips Suitable to freeze.
This recipe can be made 2 weeks ahead.

rich chocolate truffles

PREPARATION TIME 20 MINUTES (plus standing time)   COOKING TIME 5 MINUTES (plus cooling time)

**200g dark chocolate,
  chopped coarsely**
2 tablespoons cream
1 tablespoon Cointreau
$^1/_3$ cup (35g) cocoa powder

1 Combine chocolate and cream in medium heatproof bowl over medium saucepan of barely simmering water; stir until smooth. Remove from heat; cool. Stir in liqueur. Cover; stand at room temperature 3 hours or until firm.

2 Roll 2 level teaspoons of the mixture into balls. Place sifted cocoa in medium bowl. Toss balls to coat in cocoa; shake away excess cocoa. Refrigerate truffles in an airtight container.

makes 20
per truffle 4g fat; 289kJ (69 cal)
tips Grand Marnier can be substituted for the Cointreau.
This recipe can be made a week ahead; roll truffles in cocoa 3 hours before serving.

chocolate panforte

PREPARATION TIME 15 MINUTES (plus standing time)
COOKING TIME 55 MINUTES (plus cooling time)

2 sheets rice paper
$^3/_4$ cup (110g) plain flour
2 tablespoons cocoa powder
$^1/_2$ teaspoon ground cinnamon
$^1/_2$ teaspoon ground ginger
$^1/_2$ cup (150g) coarsely chopped glacé figs
$^1/_2$ cup (85g) dates, halved
$^1/_2$ cup (125g) coarsely chopped glacé peaches
$^1/_4$ cup (50g) red glacé cherries, halved
$^1/_4$ cup (50g) green glacé cherries, halved
$^1/_2$ cup (80g) blanched almonds, toasted
$^1/_2$ cup (75g) unsalted cashews, toasted
$^1/_2$ cup (75g) hazelnuts, toasted
$^1/_2$ cup (75g) macadamia nuts, toasted
$^1/_3$ cup (115g) honey
$^1/_3$ cup (75g) caster sugar
$^1/_3$ cup (75g) firmly packed brown sugar
2 tablespoons water
100g dark chocolate, melted

1   Preheat oven to moderately slow. Grease 20cm sandwich pan;
    line base with rice paper sheets.
2   Sift flour, cocoa and spices into large bowl; stir in fruit and nuts.
    Combine honey, sugars and the water in small saucepan; stir
    over heat, without boiling, until sugar dissolves. Simmer,
    uncovered, without stirring, 5 minutes. Pour hot syrup, then
    chocolate, into nut mixture; stir until well combined. Press
    mixture firmly into prepared pan. Bake in moderately slow oven
    about 45 minutes; cool in pan.
3   Remove panforte from pan; wrap in foil. Stand overnight; cut
    into thin wedges to serve.

makes 30
per wedge 7.2g fat; 741kJ (117 cal)

mini florentines

PREPARATION TIME 45 MINUTES   COOKING TIME 30 MINUTES (plus cooling time)

30g butter
2 tablespoons brown sugar
1 teaspoon golden syrup
¹/₄ teaspoon ground ginger
1 tablespoon plain flour
2 teaspoons mixed peel
1 tablespoon finely chopped red
   glacé cherries
¹/₄ cup (20g) flaked almonds,
   chopped coarsely
75g dark chocolate

1 Preheat oven to moderate. Combine butter, sugar and syrup in small saucepan; stir over heat, without boiling, until sugar dissolves. Remove from heat.

2 Stir in ginger and flour, then mixed peel, cherries and nuts. Drop level ½ teaspoons of mixture onto greased oven trays, leaving about 6cm between each to allow mixture to spread. Cook only six at a time.

3 Bake in moderate oven about 5 minutes or until golden brown; gently push florentines into shape with a small cutter or palette knife while still hot. Stand florentines 1 minute before transferring to wire rack to cool.

4 Melt chocolate; spread chocolate over flat side of florentines; run a fork through chocolate, before it sets, to make a wavy pattern. Stand florentines, chocolate-side up, on wire rack until set.

makes 36
per florentine 1.6g fat; 108kJ (26 cal)
tip This recipe can be made 3 days ahead and stored in an airtight container.

walnut brownie bites

PREPARATION TIME **15 MINUTES (plus standing time)**   COOKING TIME **20 MINUTES (plus cooling time)**

$^1/_2$ **cup (50g) walnuts, toasted,**
   chopped finely
80g butter
150g dark chocolate,
   chopped coarsely
$^3/_4$ **cup (150g) firmly packed**
   brown sugar
1 egg, beaten lightly
$^1/_3$ **cup (50g) plain flour**
$^1/_4$ **cup (60g) sour cream**
3 x 50g packet Rolos

1   Preheat oven to moderate. Lightly grease two non-stick 12-hole
1½-tablespoon (30ml) mini muffin pans; divide walnut among holes.

2   Stir butter and chocolate in small saucepan over low heat until smooth.
Stir in sugar; cool to just warm.

3   Stir in egg, then flour and sour cream; spoon mixture into prepared pan.
Press one Rolo into centre of each quantity of mixture; spread mixture
so that Rolo is completely enclosed. Bake in moderate oven 15 minutes.
Using a sharp-pointed knife, loosen sides of brownies from pan; stand
10 minutes. Remove brownies gently from pan.

makes 24
per brownie   8.9g fat; 607kJ (145 cal)
tip These treats are best served while still warm.

pistachio bread

PREPARATION TIME **10 MINUTES** (plus standing time)
COOKING TIME **45 MINUTES** (plus cooling time)

3 egg whites
$^1/_3$ cup (75g) sugar
$^1/_4$ teaspoon ground cardamom
1 teaspoon finely grated orange rind
$^3/_4$ cup (110g) plain flour
$^3/_4$ cup (110g) shelled pistachios

1 Preheat oven to moderate. Grease 8cm x 26cm bar pan; line base
   and sides with baking paper, extending paper 2cm above long
   sides of pan.
2 Beat egg whites in small bowl with electric mixer until soft peaks
   form. With motor operating, gradually add sugar, beating until
   dissolved between additions. Fold in cardamom, rind, flour and
   nuts; spread bread mixture into prepared pan.
3 Bake in moderate oven about 30 minutes or until browned lightly;
   cool in pan. Wrap in foil; stand overnight.
4 Preheat oven to slow.
5 Using a serrated or electric knife, cut bread on an angle into 3mm
   slices. Place slices on ungreased oven trays. Bake in slow oven
   about 15 minutes or until dry and crisp; turn onto wire rack to cool.

makes 35 slices
per slice 1.6g fat; 158kJ (38 cal)
tips Uncut bread can be frozen after the first baking.
After the second baking, bread slices can be stored up to
4 days in an airtight container.
For a different spiced version, substitute the cardamom with
½ teaspoon ground cinnamon and ¼ teaspoon ground nutmeg.

sugared pastry twists

PREPARATION TIME **5 MINUTES**   COOKING TIME **15 MINUTES**

1 sheet ready-rolled puff pastry, thawed
1 egg white
3 teaspoons caster sugar
$\frac{1}{2}$ teaspoon ground cinnamon

1 Preheat oven to moderate.

2 Brush pastry with egg white; sprinkle evenly with combined sugar and cinnamon.

3 Using a fluted pastry wheel, cut pastry sheet in half. Cut each half crossways into 5mm strips.

4 Twist each pastry strip; place on lightly greased oven tray. Bake in moderate oven about 15 minutes or until pastry browns lightly.

makes 96
per twist 0.4g fat; 30kJ (7 cal)

caramel chocolate tarts

PREPARATION TIME 25 MINUTES (plus standing time)
COOKING TIME 15 MINUTES (plus cooling time)

1 cup (150g) plain flour
90g butter, chopped
¼ cup (55g) caster sugar
100g dark chocolate, melted

CARAMEL FILLING

395g can sweetened condensed milk
30g butter, chopped
2 tablespoons golden syrup

1   Preheat oven to moderate. Grease two 12-hole 1½-tablespoon (30ml) mini muffin pans.
2   Sift flour into medium bowl. Rub in butter; stir in sugar. Press 2 teaspoons of the mixture into each hole of muffin pans. Bake in moderate oven about 10 minutes or until browned lightly.
3   Pour hot caramel filling over hot bases; return to oven 3 minutes. Stand tarts 2 minutes before gently removing from pans; cool.
4   Spread top of tarts with chocolate; stand at room temperature until set.

caramel filling   Combine ingredients in small saucepan; stir over low heat until butter melts and mixture is combined.

makes 24
per tart   6.9g fat; 623kJ (149 cal)
tips   Caramel filling and chocolate suitable to microwave. This recipe can be made 3 days ahead and stored in an airtight container.

greek almond biscuits

PREPARATION TIME 30 MINUTES   COOKING TIME 15 MINUTES (plus cooling time)

3 cups (375g) almond meal
1 cup (220g) caster sugar
3 drops almond essence
3 egg whites, beaten lightly
1 cup (80g) flaked almonds

1 Preheat oven to moderate.

2 Combine almond meal, sugar and essence in large bowl. Add egg whites; stir until mixture forms a firm paste.

3 Roll level tablespoons of the mixture into flaked almonds; roll into 8cm logs. Press on remaining almonds. Shape logs to form crescents; place on baking paper-lined oven trays. Bake in moderate oven about 15 minutes or until browned lightly; cool on trays.

makes 25
per biscuit 10.1g fat; 595kJ (142 cal)
tip Biscuits can be made a week ahead and are suitable to freeze.

portuguese custard tarts

PREPARATION TIME 25 MINUTES (plus thawing time)   COOKING TIME 30 MINUTES (plus cooling time)

4 egg yolks
¹/₂ cup (110g) caster sugar
2 tablespoons cornflour
1 cup (250ml) cream
¹/₂ cup (125ml) water
strip of lemon rind
2 teaspoons vanilla essence
1 sheet ready-rolled butter puff pastry

1 Preheat oven to hot. Grease a 12-hole ¹/₃-cup (80ml) muffin pan. Place egg yolks, sugar and cornflour in medium saucepan; whisk until combined. Gradually whisk in cream and the water until smooth.

2 Add rind; stir over medium heat until mixture just comes to a boil. Remove from heat immediately. Remove rind; stir in essence.

3 Cut pastry sheet in half. Remove plastic; stack halves on top of each other. Stand about 5 minutes or until thawed. Roll pastry up tightly, from the short side; cut log into 12 x 1cm rounds.

4 Lay pastry, cut-side up, on lightly floured board; roll each round out to about 10cm. Press rounds into prepared muffin pans with fingers. Spoon custard into pastry cases.

5 Bake tarts in hot oven about 20 minutes or until well browned. Transfer to wire rack to cool.

makes 12
per tart 14.1g fat; 831kJ (198 cal)
tip This recipe is best made on the day of serving.

glossary

all-bran a low-fat, high-fibre breakfast cereal based on wheat bran.

allspice also known as pimento or jamaican pepper; available whole or ground. Tastes like a blend of cinnamon, cloves and nutmeg.

almonds flat, pointed-ended nuts with pitted brown shell enclosing a creamy white kernel which is covered by a brown skin.

blanched brown skins removed.

flaked paper-thin slices.

meal also known as ground almonds; nuts are powdered to a coarse flour texture, for use in baking or as a thickening agent.

slivered small lengthways-cut pieces.

sugared also known as vienna almonds. Toffee-coated nuts.

arborio rice small, round-grain rice well suited to absorb a large amount of liquid; especially suitable for risottos.

bacardi white rum.

bacon rashers slices of bacon; made from pork side, cured and smoked.

bamboo shoots the young shoots of bamboo plants; available fresh and in cans.

basil, thai also known as horapa, is different from holy basil and sweet basil in both look and taste. Having smaller leaves and purplish stems, thai basil has a slight liquorice or aniseed taste, and is one of the basic flavours that typify Thai cuisine.

bean thread noodles also known as bean thread vermicelli or cellophane noodles.

beetroot also known as red beets; firm, round root vegetable.

besan a flour made from ground chickpeas. It is used as a thickener and as a main ingredient in Indian cooking.

bicarbonate of soda (baking soda) the acid and alkaline combination, when moistened and heated, gives off carbon dioxide which aerates and lightens the mixture during baking.

black onion seeds also known as kolonji or nigella.

baby bok choy
bok choy

bok choy also known as bak choy, pak choy, chinese white cabbage and chinese chard, has a mild mustard taste. Use stems and leaves. Baby bok choy is smaller and more tender than bok choy.

breadcrumbs

packaged fine-textured, crunchy, purchased, white breadcrumbs.

stale one- or two-day-old bread made into crumbs by grating, blending or processing.

butter use salted or unsalted (sweet) butter; 125g is equal to 1 stick butter.

butter beans cans labelled butter beans are, in fact, cannellini beans. Confusingly butter is also another name for lima beans, sold both dried and canned; a large beige bean having a mealy texture and mild taste.

buttermilk sold alongside all fresh milk products in supermarkets; despite the implication of its name, is low in fat.

cajun seasoning used to give an authentic USA Deep South spicy cajun flavour to food, this packaged blend of assorted herbs and spices can include paprika, basil, onion, fennel, thyme, cayenne and tarragon.

capers
caperberries

caperberries are the fruit of the same Mediterranean shrub that produces the small flowerbuds we know as capers. About the size of a small olive, they are sold pickled in vinegar; rinse and drain before use.

capers the grey-green buds of a warm climate (usually Mediterranean) shrub, sold either dried and salted or pickled in a vinegar brine. We used the pickled variety.

capsicum also known as bell pepper or, simply, pepper; membranes and seeds should be discarded before use.

cardamom native to India and used extensively in its cuisine; can be purchased in pod, seed or ground form. Has a distinctive aromatic, sweetly rich flavour.

cayenne pepper a thin-fleshed, long, extremely hot red chilli; usually purchased dried and ground.

cheese

bocconcini walnut-sized baby mozzarella. Spoils rapidly; keep refrigerated, in brine, for 1 to 2 days only.

brie smooth and voluptuous, brie has a bloomy white rind and a creamy centre which becomes runnier as it ripens.

cheddar the most widely eaten cheese in the world, cheddar is a semi-hard cow milk cheese. It ranges in colour from white to pale yellow and has a slightly crumbly texture if properly matured.

cottage fresh, white, unripened curd cheese with a grainy consistency.

fetta a white cheese with milky, fresh acidity. Most commonly made from cow's milk, though sheep and goat milk varieties are available. Fetta is sometimes described as a pickled cheese because it is matured in brine for at least a month, which imparts a strong salty flavour. Fetta is solid but crumbles readily.

goat made from goat's milk, has an earthy, strong taste; available both soft and firm.

grated pizza a commercial blend of varying proportions of processed grated mozzarella, cheddar and parmesan.

haloumi a firm, cream-coloured sheep milk cheese matured in brine; somewhat like a salty fetta in flavour, it can be grilled or fried, briefly, without breaking down.

mascarpone is a cultured cream product. Whitish to creamy yellow in colour, it has a soft, creamy texture, a fat content of 75%, and a slightly tangy taste.

mozzarella a semi-soft cheese with a delicate, fresh taste; has a low melting point and stringy texture when hot.

parmesan also known as parmigiano, is a hard, grainy cheese. The curd is salted in brine for a month before being aged for up to two years in humid conditions.

pecorino is the generic Italian name for cheeses made from sheep's milk. It's a hard, white to pale yellow cheese, usually matured for 8 to 12 months.

ricotta a sweet, fairly moist, fresh curd cheese having a low fat content.

chickpeas also called garbanzos, hummus or channa; an irregularly round, sandy-coloured legume.

chilli flakes crushed dried chillies.

chilli powder the Asian variety is the hottest, made from ground chillies; it can be used as a substitute for fresh chillies in the proportion of ½ teaspoon ground chilli powder to 1 medium chopped fresh chilli.

chinese broccoli also known as gai larn. Every part of chinese broccoli is edible.

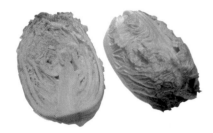

chinese cabbage also known as peking or napa cabbage, wong bok and petsai, the pale green, crinkly leaves of this elongated cabbage only require brief cooking.

chinese rice wine made from rice wine lees, salt and alcohol; replace with a pale dry sherry if unavailable.

choy sum also known as flowering bok choy, flowering white, or chinese flowering, cabbage. The stems, leaves and yellow flowers are served steamed, stir-fried and in soups.

ciabatta a crusty Italian loaf.

citron vodka citrus-flavoured vodka.

clams also known as vongole.

cocoa powder also known as cocoa; dried, unsweetened, roasted ground cocoa beans.

coconut

cream the first pressing from grated mature coconut flesh; available in cans and cartons.

flaked dried, flaked coconut flesh.

milk the second pressing (less rich) from grated mature coconut flesh; available in cans and cartons.

cointreau citrus-flavoured liqueur.

cornflour also known as cornstarch; used as a thickening agent in cooking.

cornmeal often called polenta, to which this ground corn (maize) is similar, albeit coarser. One can be substituted for the other, but textures will vary.

couscous a fine, grain-like cereal product, made from semolina.

crab stick made from processed Alaskan pollack flavoured with crab.

cream

double (minimum fat content 54%) thick, not for whipping.

fresh (minimum fat content 35%) also known as pure cream and pouring cream; contains no additives.

thickened (minimum fat content 35%) whipping cream containing a thickener.

curry leaves shiny, sharp-ended, green leaves used, fresh or dried, like bay leaves, in cooking, especially in Indian curries.

curry powder a blend of ground spices used for convenience when making Indian food. Can consist of some of the following spices in varying proportions: dried chilli, cinnamon, coriander, cumin, fennel, fenugreek, mace, cardamom and turmeric. Choose mild or hot to suit your taste.

custard powder packaged vanilla pudding mixture; combine with milk or water to produce pouring custard.

daikon a basic food in Japan, it is also called the giant white radish. A long, white horseradish with a wonderful, sweet flavour.

drinking chocolate sweetened cocoa powder to mix with milk.

egg noodles made from wheat flour and eggs; strands vary in thickness.

eggplant also known as aubergine.

essence also known as extract.

fish sauce also called nam pla or nuoc nam; made from pulverised salted fermented fish, most often anchovies. Has a pungent smell and strong taste; use sparingly.

five-spice powder a fragrant mixture of ground cinnamon, cloves, star anise, sichuan pepper and fennel seeds.

flour

buckwheat although not a true cereal, flour is made from its seeds. Available from health food stores.

plain an all-purpose flour, made from wheat.

self-raising plain flour sifted with baking powder in the proportion of 1 cup flour to 2 teaspoons baking powder.

wholemeal plain also known as all-purpose wholewheat flour; no baking powder added.

frangelico hazelnut-flavoured liqueur.

french-trimmed lamb cutlets all the fat and gristle at the narrow end of the bone has been removed.

galangal also known as laos. It looks like ginger but is dense and fibrous and much harder to cut. Galangal adds a distinctive peppery flavour to food. If using in pieces, remove from the dish before serving.

garam masala a blend of spices, originating in North India; based on varying proportions of cardamom, cinnamon, cloves, coriander, fennel and cumin, roasted and ground together. Black pepper and chilli can be added for a hotter version.

gelatine we used powdered gelatine. It is also available in sheet form (leaf gelatine).

ghee clarified butter; with the milk solids removed, this fat can be heated to a high temperature without burning.

ginger also known as green or root ginger; the thick gnarled root of a tropical plant. Can be kept, peeled, covered with dry sherry in a jar and refrigerated, or frozen in an airtight container.

glacé cherries are cooked in heavy sugar syrup and then dried.

glucose syrup also known as liquid glucose, made from wheat starch; used in jam and confectionery and available at health food stores and supermarkets.

golden syrup a by-product of refined sugarcane; pure maple syrup or honey can be substituted.

grand marnier orange-flavoured liqueur based on cognac brandy.

green ginger wine beverage 14% alcohol by volume, has the taste of fresh ginger. Substitute dry (white) vermouth, if preferred.

hazelnut meal also known as ground hazelnuts; nuts are powdered to a coarse flour texture.

hazelnuts also known as filberts; plump, grape-sized, rich, sweet nuts having a brown inedible skin removed by rubbing heated nuts together vigorously in a tea towel.

herbs we have specified when to use fresh or dried herbs. We used dried (not ground) herbs in the proportion of 1:4 for fresh herbs; use 1 teaspoon dried herbs instead of 4 teaspoons (1 tablespoon) chopped fresh herbs.

hoisin sauce a thick, sweet and spicy Chinese paste made from salted fermented soy beans, onions and garlic.

hokkien noodles also known as stir-fry noodles; fresh wheat-flour noodles resembling thick, yellow-brown spaghetti. Must be rinsed under hot water to remove starch and excess oil before use.

jasmine rice a fragrant long-grained rice; white rice can be substituted but will not taste the same.

kaffir lime leaves aromatic leaves of a small citrus tree bearing a wrinkled-skinned yellow-green fruit.

kahlúa coffee-flavoured liqueur.

washed

unwashed

kipfler potato long, oval-shaped potato that has golden skin and waxy, yellow flesh.

kiwi fruit also known as chinese gooseberry.

kumara Polynesian name of orange-fleshed sweet potato often confused with yam.

lamb drumsticks also known as frenched shanks or trimmed shanks, these are lamb shanks with the gristle at the narrow end of the bone removed and the bone trimmed.

lavash flat, unleavened bread.

lebanese cucumber small, slender and thin-skinned, with juicy flesh and tiny seeds.

lemon grass a tall, clumping, lemon-smelling and tasting, sharp-edged grass; use only the white lower part of each stem.

lentils (red, brown, yellow) dried pulses often identified by their colour.

macadamia rich and buttery nut; store in refrigerator because of high oil content.

madeira a fortified wine originally from the Portuguese island of the same name. Types range from golden and dry to rich, sweet and dark; can be served as an aperitif but is also an excellent cooking wine.

malibu coconut-flavoured rum.

maple syrup a thin syrup distilled from the sap of the maple tree. Maple-flavoured syrup or pancake syrup is not an adequate substitute for the real thing.

marsala a sweet, fortified wine.

mesclun a gourmet salad mix of assorted young lettuce and other green leaves, including baby spinach, mizuna and curly endive.

mexican-style beans a canned mixture of either haricot or pinto beans cooked with tomato, peppers, onion, garlic and spices.

mince also known as ground meat.

mirin a Japanese champagne-coloured cooking wine made of glutinous rice and alcohol; not to be confused with sake, the Japanese rice wine made for drinking. There is a seasoned sweet mirin called manjo mirin that is made of water, rice, corn syrup and alcohol.

mixed peel candied citrus peel.

mushrooms

button small, cultivated white mushrooms with a mild flavour.

flat large, flat mushrooms with a rich earthy flavour. They are sometimes misnamed field mushrooms which are wild mushrooms.

shiitake also known as chinese black, forest or golden oak mushrooms, have a unique meaty flavour popular in Asia. Often sold dried, soak to rehydrate before use.

straw a cultivated Chinese variety with an earthy flavour, usually sold canned in brine. Substitute canned champignons or fresh baby button mushrooms.

swiss brown light to dark brown mushrooms with full-bodied flavour also known as roman. If unavailable, you can substitute button mushrooms.

mustard

black seeds also known as brown mustard seeds; more pungent than the white (or yellow) seeds used in prepared mustards.

dijon a pale brown, distinctively flavoured, fairly mild French mustard.

seeded also known as wholegrain. A French-style coarse-grain mustard made from crushed mustard seeds and dijon-style French mustard.

nori a type of dried seaweed used in Japanese cooking as a flavouring, garnish or for sushi. Sold in thin sheets.

oil

chilli made by steeping red chillies in vegetable oil; intensely hot in flavour.

macadamia made from ground macadamias.

olive made from ripened olives. Extra virgin and virgin are the best, while extra light or light refers to taste not fat levels.

peanut pressed from ground peanuts; most commonly used oil in Asian cooking because of its high smoke point.

sesame made from roasted, crushed white sesame seeds. Do not use for frying.

vegetable any of a number of oils sourced from plants rather than animal fats.

onion

green also known as scallion or (incorrectly) shallot; an immature onion picked before the bulb has formed, having a long, bright-green edible stalk.

red also known as spanish, red spanish or bermuda onion; a sweet-flavoured, large, purple-red onion.

oyster sauce Asian in origin, this rich brown sauce is made from oysters and their brine, cooked with salt and soy sauce, and thickened with starches.

paprika ground dried red capsicum (bell pepper), available sweet or hot.

pecan a golden-brown, buttery, rich nut.

pide turkish bread that comes in long (about 45cm) flat loaves as well as rounds; made from wheat flour and sprinkled with sesame or black onion seeds.

pine nuts also known as pignoli; small, cream-coloured kernels obtained from the cones of different varieties of pine trees.

pistachio pale green, delicately flavoured nut inside a hard off-white shell. To peel, soak shelled nuts in boiling water 5 minutes; drain, then pat dry with absorbent paper. Rub skins with cloth to peel.

pitta pocket bread small flat pieces of lebanese bread that separate into two thin rounds to form a pocket.

polenta a flour-like cereal made of ground corn (maize); similar to cornmeal but finer in texture; also the name of the dish made from it.

prawns also known as shrimps.

prosciutto salt-cured, air-dried (unsmoked) pressed ham; usually sold in paper-thin slices, ready to eat.

pumpkin sometimes used interchangeably with the word squash.

raisins dried sweet grapes.

red curry paste is a combination of dried red chillies, onions, garlic, oil, lemon rind, shrimp paste, ground cumin, paprika, ground turmeric and ground black pepper.

rice noodles dried noodles made from rice flour and water, available flat and wide or very thin (vermicelli). Should be soaked in boiling water to soften. Also known as rice stick noodles.

rice noodles, fresh soft white noodles made from rice flour and vegetable oil; available in varying thicknesses from vermicelli thin to broad flat. Must be rinsed under hot water to remove starch and excess oil before use.

rice paper wrappers, dried made from ground rice flour, salt and water; imported from Southeast Asia. Sold packaged in 375g batches in round or square pieces.

rice paper a fine, edible paper used in the making of biscuits. It is not actually made from rice, but from the pith of a small tree which grows in Asia. It can be found in specialist food stores and delicatessens.

rocket also known as arugula, rugula and rucola; a peppery-tasting green leaf which can be used similarly to baby spinach leaves, eaten raw in salad or used in cooking. Baby rocket leaves are both smaller and less peppery.

rockmelon cantaloupe.

rolos soft caramel-filled chocolates.

roti sometimes known as chapati, is an unleavened flat bread used in place of cutlery to pick up wet curries when eating an Indian meal.

scallops a bivalve mollusc with fluted shell valve; we use scallops which still have the coral (roe) attached.

semi-dried tomatoes partially dehydrated tomatoes in oil.

sherry fortified wine consumed as an aperitif or used in cooking. Sold as fino (light, dry), amontillado (medium sweet, dark) and oloroso (full-bodied, very dark).

shrimp paste also known as trasi and blanchan; a strong-scented, almost solid preserved paste made of salted dried shrimp. Used as a pungent flavouring in many Southeast Asian soups and sauces.

snow peas also called mange tout ("eat all"). Snow pea tendrils, the growing shoots of the plant, are sold by greengrocers.

soy sauce made from fermented soy beans. Several variations are available in most supermarkets and Asian food stores.

spinach also known as english spinach or, incorrectly, silverbeet. Tender green leaves are good raw in salads or added to soups, stir-fries and stews just before serving.

sponge finger biscuits also known as savoy biscuits, lady's fingers or savoiardi biscuits, they are Italian-style crisp fingers made from sponge cake mixture.

spring roll wrappers sometimes called egg roll wrappers; they come in various sizes and can be purchased fresh or frozen from Asian supermarkets. Made from a delicate wheat-based pastry, they can be used to make gow gees and samosas as well.

sprouts tender new growths of assorted beans and seeds germinated for

consumption in salads and stir-fries. The most readily available are mung bean, soy bean, alfalfa and snow pea sprouts.

squid a type of mollusc; also known as calamari. Buy squid hoods to make preparation easier.

stock available in cans, tetra packs, cubes and powder. As a guide, 1 teaspoon of stock powder or 1 small crumbled stock cube mixed with 1 cup (250ml) water will give a fairly strong stock.

sugar snap peas also known as honey snap peas; snow peas can be substituted.

sugar

brown a soft, fine granulated sugar retaining molasses for its characteristic colour.

caster also known as superfine or finely granulated table sugar.

icing sugar mixture also known as confectioners' sugar or powdered sugar; crushed granulated sugar with a small amount of cornflour added.

pure icing sugar also known as confectioners' sugar or powdered sugar, but without the addition of cornflour.

raw natural brown granulated sugar.

sweet chilli sauce a comparatively mild, Thai-style sauce made from red chillies, sugar, garlic and vinegar.

sweetened condensed milk milk from which 60% of the water has been removed; the milk is then sweetened with sugar.

tahini sesame paste.

tandoori paste consisting of garlic, tamarind, ginger, coriander, chilli and spices.

teriyaki sauce a commercially bottled sauce usually made from soy sauce, mirin, sugar, ginger and other spices; it imparts a distinctive glaze brushed on grilled meat.

thai chillies small, hot chillies, bright red to dark green in colour.

tia maria coffee-flavoured liqueur.

tomato paste triple-concentrated tomato puree used to flavour soups, stews, sauces and casseroles.

tomato puree canned pureed tomatoes (not tomato paste). Substitute with fresh peeled and pureed tomatoes.

tomato sauce also known as ketchup or catsup; a condiment based on tomatoes, vinegar and various spices.

tortillas thin, round unleavened bread made from wheat flour or from corn.

turmeric a member of the ginger family, its root is dried and ground, resulting in the rich yellow powder that gives many Indian dishes their characteristic colour. It is intensely pungent in taste but not hot.

tzatziki greek yogurt and cucumber dish sometimes containing mint and/or garlic.

unprocessed bran made from the husks of wheat, rice or oats.

vanilla bean dried, long, thin pod from a tropical golden orchid; the minuscule black seeds inside the bean impart a luscious vanilla flavour in baking and desserts.

vindaloo curry paste a fiery paste consisting of coriander, cumin, turmeric, chilli, ginger, garlic, tamarind and lentil flour.

vinegar

balsamic authentic only from the province of Modena, Italy; aged in antique wooden casks to give the exquisite pungent flavour.

brown made from fermented malt and beech shavings.

cider made from fermented apples.

raspberry made from fresh raspberries steeped in a white wine vinegar.

rice a colourless vinegar made from fermented rice and flavoured with sugar and salt. Also known as seasoned rice vinegar.

sherry natural vinegar aged in oak according to the traditional Spanish system.

white made from spirit of cane sugar.

wasabi an Asian horseradish used to make the pungent, green-coloured sauce traditionally served with Japanese raw fish dishes; sold in powdered or paste form.

white chocolate we used eating chocolate.

wonton wrappers gow gee, egg or spring roll pastry sheets can be substituted.

yellow patty-pan squash round squash with a frilled edge, also available in green.

zucchini also known as courgette.

index

facts and figures

Wherever you live, you'll be able to use our recipes with the help of these easy-to-follow conversions. While these conversions are approximate only, the difference between an exact and the approximate conversion of various liquid and dry measures is but minimal and will not affect your cooking results.

dry measures

metric	imperial
15g	1/2oz
30g	1oz
60g	2oz
90g	3oz
125g	4oz (1/4lb)
155g	5oz
185g	6oz
220g	7oz
250g	8oz (1/2lb)
280g	9oz
315g	10oz
345g	11oz
375g	12oz (3/4lb)
410g	13oz
440g	14oz
470g	15oz
500g	16oz (1lb)
750g	24oz (1 1/2lb)
1kg	32oz (2lb)

liquid measures

metric	imperial
30ml	1 fluid oz
60ml	2 fluid oz
100ml	3 fluid oz
125ml	4 fluid oz
150ml	5 fluid oz (1/4 pint/1 gill)
190ml	6 fluid oz
250ml	8 fluid oz
300ml	10 fluid oz (1/2 pint)
500ml	16 fluid oz
600ml	20 fluid oz (1 pint)
1000ml (1 litre)	1 3/4 pints

helpful measures

metric	imperial
3mm	1/8in
6mm	1/4in
1cm	1/2in
2cm	3/4in
2.5cm	1in
5cm	2in
6cm	2 1/2in
8cm	3in
10cm	4in
13cm	5in
15cm	6in
18cm	7in
20cm	8in
23cm	9in
25cm	10in
28cm	11in
30cm	12in (1ft)

measuring equipment

The difference between one country's measuring cups and another's is, at most, within a 2 or 3 teaspoon variance. (For the record, one Australian metric measuring cup holds approximately 250ml.) The most accurate way of measuring dry ingredients is to weigh them. When measuring liquids, use a clear glass or plastic jug with the metric markings. (One Australian metric tablespoon holds 20ml; one Australian metric teaspoon holds 5ml.)

Note: North America, NZ and the UK use 15ml tablespoons. All cup and spoon measurements are level.

We use large eggs having an average weight of 60g.

how to measure

When using graduated metric measuring cups, shake dry ingredients loosely into the appropriate cup. Do not tap the cup on a bench or tightly pack the ingredients unless directed to do so. Level top of measuring cups and measuring spoons with a knife. When measuring liquids, place a clear glass or plastic jug with metric markings on a flat surface to check accuracy at eye level.

oven temperatures

These oven temperatures are only a guide. Always check the manufacturer's manual.

	°C (Celsius)	°F (Fahrenheit)	Gas Mark
Very slow	120	250	1
Slow	150	300	2
Moderately slow	160	325	3
Moderate	180 – 190	350 – 375	4
Moderately hot	200 – 210	400 – 425	5
Hot	220 – 230	450 – 475	6
Very hot	240 – 250	500 – 525	7

Editors *Deborah Quick, Lynda Wilton*
Designer *Caryl Wiggins*
Food editor *Louise Patniotis*
Special feature photographer *Andre Martin*
Special feature stylist *Jane Hann*
Special feature home economist *Cathie Lonnie*
Food director *Pamela Clark*

ACP Books Staff
Editorial director *Susan Tomnay*
Creative director *Hieu Chi Nguyen*
Editorial coordinator *Holly van Oyen*
Editorial assistant *Lana Meldrum*
Publishing manager (sales) *Jennifer McDonald*
Publishing manager (rights & new projects) *Jane Hazell*
Brand manager *Donna Gianniotis*
Pre-press *Harry Palmer*
Production manager *Carol Currie*
Business manager *Sally Lees*
Chief executive officer *John Alexander*
Group publisher *Jill Baker*
Publisher *Sue Wannan*

Produced by ACP books, Sydney.
Printing by Leefung-Asco, China.
Published by ACP Publishing Pty Limited,
54 Park St, Sydney; GPO Box 4088, Sydney, NSW 1028.
Ph: (02) 9282 8618 Fax: (02) 9267 9438.
acpbooks@acp.com.au
www.acpbooks.com.au

To order books phone 136 116.
Send recipe enquiries to
reccipeenquiries@acp.com.au

AUSTRALIA: Distributed by Network Services,
GPO Box 4088, Sydney, NSW 1028.
Ph: (02) 9282 8777 Fax: (02) 9264 3278.
UNITED KINGDOM: Distributed by Australian Consolidated
Press (UK), Moulton Park Business Centre, Red House Rd,
Moulton Park, Northampton, NN3 6AQ
Ph: (01604) 497 531 Fax: (01604) 497 533 acpukltd@aol.com
CANADA: Distributed by Whitecap Books Ltd, 351 Lynn Ave,
North Vancouver, BC, V7J 2C4
Ph: (604) 980 9852 Fax: (604) 980 8197
customerservice@whitecap.ca www.whitecap.ca
NEW ZEALAND: Distributed by Netlink Distribution Company,
Level 4, 23 Hargreaves St, College Hill, Auckland 1,
Ph: (9) 302 7616.

Great Casual Food
Includes index.
ISBN 1 86396 297 2
1.Cookery. 2. Quick and easy cookery.
I. Title: Australian Women's Weekly.
641.5
© ACP Publishing Pty Limited 2003
ABN 18 053 273 546
This publication is copyright. No part of it may be
reproduced or transmitted in any form without the
written permission of the publishers.

Photographers: *Alan Benson, Scott Cameron, Robert Clark, Gerry Colley, Brett Danton, Joe Filshie, Rowan Fotheringham, Ashley Mackevicius, Andre Martin, Mark O'Meara, Rob Shaw, Brett Stevens, Robert Taylor, Ian Wallace.*

Stylists: *Frances Abdallaoui, Wendy Berecry, Clare Bradford, Marie-Helene Clauzon, Jane Collins, Georgina Dolling, Carolyn Fienberg, Kay Francis, Jane Hann, Katy Holder, Cherise Koch, Vicki Liley, Janet Mitchell, Michelle Noerianto, Sarah O'Brien, Sophia Young.*

Cover: Lamb cutlets with potato and parsnip mash, page 106
Photographer: Andre Martin
Stylist: Jane Hann

Back cover: Buttermilk pancakes with ricotta cream, page 24
Photographer: Andre Martin
Stylist: Jane Hann